SUSILA
BUDHI
DHARMA

MUHAMMAD SUBUH
SUMOHADIWIDJOJO

Published in Great Britain in 1991 by
Subud Publications International Ltd
Southdown House, Golden Cross, near Hailsham,
E Sussex, BN27 4AH, England

Copyright © 1959 the family of Bapak Muhammad Subuh
Sumohadiwidjojo

First published 1959
Reprinted 1975 with a new English translation
Third edition, 1991

ISBN 1 869822 11 0

Designed by Marcus Bolt
Typeset by Selectmove Ltd, London
Printed by Biddles of Guildford

PUBLISHER'S NOTE

Susila Budhi Dharma is the most important and comprehensive statement made by Bapak Muhammad Subuh Sumohadiwidjojo on the worship of God through the *latihan kejiwaan* of Subud, and on the meaning and purpose of Subud for the life of mankind on earth. Bapak was the founder of the spiritual movement called Subud (an abbreviation of *Susila, Budhi, Dharma*), in Indonesia in 1947. Subud has since spread to most countries of the world.

In a talk in Vancouver in 1981 Bapak referred to *Susila Budhi Dharma*:

In the holy books it is said that man's journey upwards through the realms of life is not something that a human being can study, research, approach by his own effort and strength. It is something that can only be done by the power of Almighty God. And the only contribution, the only attitude, that a human being can have in this is surrender with acceptance and sincerity towards God's power.

If you really examine and measure, step by step, the levels and the journey that have to be gone through from where we are, from the lowest to the highest, how many hundred million years would it take to complete that journey to heaven?

Something has been told about that journey in *Susila Budhi Dharma*. Those of you who are able to feel it, those of you who are able to receive it, have a look at that book. Read it, and maybe it will make you able just to grasp, or grope towards, something in that direction. It will give you an idea of this journey, from the bottom as it goes upwards.

Susila Budhi Dharma was originally received by Bapak in High Javanese and later rendered by him into Indonesian – not a straight translation but an amplification of the High Javanese text. Both texts were published together with an English translation of the Indonesian by SPI in Britain in 1959, and reprinted by SPI in 1972 with a revised English translation.

This present edition carries only the 1972 English translation; for reasons of economy, the Javanese and Indonesian texts have not been included.

Susila Budhi Dharma was received and written down by Bapak as a sung poem. Each chapter was sung to a different traditional Javanese melody, the name of which gives the chapters their title in this edition. The verses in this edition are numbered for easier reference to the original.

A few of the words have been left in the Indonesian because they do not have an exact English equivalent.

About the *latihan kejiwaan* of Subud, Bapak has said,

These spiritual exercises of Subud are in truth worship of man towards God, awakened in us by the power of God at the moment this same power arrests the interference of our thinking minds, our hearts and desires. This means that the spiritual exercise that we have received has been awakened in us only by the will of the One Almighty God of our worship. Since the exercise comes from God and by the will of God, it follows that this, of itself, will lead us towards God Who wills it to be so. And since all this comes by the will of God, we can be certain that the principles of the spiritual exercise are in accordance with what is intended by God for mankind as a whole.

The qualities needed by man in order to receive the gift of God in the right way are symbolised by the [Sanskrit] words *Susila, Budhi, Dharma*.

Susila denotes those qualities which give rise to a character, conduct and actions which are truly human, and in accordance with the will of God.

Budhi means that in all creatures, including man, there dwells an inner force to draw us towards our proper path, the path that leads to God.

Dharma signifies sincerity, surrender and submission to God, which are awakened in man by the will of God Himself.

These are the qualities of a man who is able to receive the commandments of God and the gifts of God, both for the needs of his life on this earth and also for his life after death. They are the very qualities bestowed by God upon man in order that he may be able fully to receive all that God has ordained concerning human life upon earth.

These principles and aims of Subud can be summed up by saying that it is God's will that we should dwell upon earth, worship God and return to God. This corresponds to the teaching of the prophets, that all creation comes from God and all returns to God again.

From *The Meaning of Subud*, SPI, London, 1959, 1991.

CONTENTS

PREFACE

To explain the contents of this book it will be best if Bapak first makes clear the conditions under which human beings can receive contact with the Great Life, whose source is in fact the Power of God Almighty.

As is evident, God is powerful and far excels man in all things; for in very truth He is the Creator of mankind and of heaven and earth. So man as he really is, then, is just a created thing, powerless before God.

Necessarily, since this is his real condition, man cannot with his heart and mind understand or reflect on the Nature and Power of God. This is why, whenever people try to find a way that may lead to contact with the Great Life, many are stranded on the path or, if not, are impelled – not having a conscious *jiwa* – to stray in other directions, directions which in reality are mirages of the imagination, heart and mind.

So man, in seeking the nature of worship that can make contact with the Great Life, needs above all to stop the welling up of his imagination and thinking. For by doing that he really paralyses his *nafsu* and surrenders his human ability and wisdom; that is to say, the human being obeys and submits with complete sincerity to God Who rules within him.

This in fact is nothing new, for men of old followed this path and found a contact of this quality that they could feel within them. Why, then, are there not many people like that in our own time who still have that contact? The reason is simply that conditions on earth for mankind keep changing as generation succeeds generation, and many people are easily affected by the influence of these ever-changing conditions that face them. Especially has this been so as the human

xi

mind has progressively developed its science. This has, as it were, increasingly opened the way for the inner feeling to fall from the realm of inner peace into the realm of thought. In consequence, the human self gradually comes to be ruled more and more by thought, instead of by the quietness of the inner feeling or the inner self, so that in the end man's emotions and brain are always busy and his inner feeling has almost no opportunity to be at peace.

Certainly men must think, for thought is an important tool with which they can strive to fulfil the needs of their life on earth and so make their existence here an orderly one. But to become aware of the *kejiwaan* and make contact again with the Great Life men do not need to use their minds. On the contrary, they should stop the process of their thinking and imagining. For only by so doing can a person receive something from beyond his reach that at length attracts a vibration of energy felt within the self. Clearly, then, the sole way to make contact with the Great Life, or with the Power of God, is for a man to surrender sincerely and earnestly. And this surrender must not be in word only, but must penetrate throughout his inner feeling until he truly feels that he believes in, praises and worships no one but God Almighty (Allah).

When he can really do this, at that moment he will also feel powerless, but with no sense of loss, and still conscious.

That is to say, he will feel powerless because at that moment the strength of his *nafsu*, heart and mind will have gone from him; and he will still feel complete because his inner feeling will then be filled with something that comes from the Great Life; finally, he will feel conscious because of the revival of his human *jiwa*.

So is it, if a man can do this in the right way. But when, in his efforts to do this, he keeps using thought because he regards it as a means or tool able to overcome everything, then he can hardly hope that it will be possible to make contact with the Great Life.

This truth was often stated by those who received while living on earth in centuries long past. They said that man's one and only way to be able to draw near to the Power of God is that he must be willing to quieten his inner feeling with complete patience, trust and sincerity.

This has been an absolute requirement, for in truth this gift from God can only be received by men who have inner feelings filled with surrender, patience, trust and sincerity before the Greatness of God.

Such are Bapak's words to all who may wish to read this book. The explanations in the pages which follow show the way of the *kejiwaan* that is found in receiving the *latihan*.

In conclusion, Bapak hopes that the inner feelings of those who read the book may be opened by God Almighty, so that they may be able to worship Him in earnest. Bapak also hopes that readers will be very forgiving if anything Bapak has said is out of place. Amen.

Bapak Muhammad Subuh Sumohadiwidjojo

1
SINOM

1. So that a certain spiritual truth, which has been received both inwardly and outwardly, may be given form and carried into effect, here its entire essence has been expressed, to beautiful melodies and metres, in the hope that the evidence that is needed may be obtained.

2. These are the words of divine counsel received and so far as was necessary written down in the historic city of Yogyakarta in the year 1952.

3. To begin with, let it be explained here that, soon after the mind has stopped thinking and has been separated from the feelings as a result of the opening, a vibration of life is felt which goes on to encompass the whole body and soon causes movements that seem very strange to the mind.

4. This state is indeed truly strange to the mind, because it is not something that thought can bring into being, but something real that can be received and witnessed by a feeling no longer influenced by thinking.

5. When you have received and witnessed this reality, go on to feel truly what in fact is happening within you. By so doing you will get an indication of the right path; moreover, the authenticity of the true inner self will become apparent.

6. Because of this, you will see what faults you have always borne – faults caused by your parents' conduct before their child came into existence.

7. This state is something truly remarkable, because – in the degree to which one can attain it – it reveals the qualities a person lacks for his status as a human being, the lack of which makes his chance of reaching higher levels, or the realm of perfection, very slight.

8. The child is truly aware of these faults, and he can do nothing but accept what has befallen his inner self. And this case, if really considered, is far from uncommon. On the contrary, it is almost everybody's experience because, in the first place, people cannot foresee what is going to happen, and secondly, in any case men are but men, whose state can easily change and who are easily affected by conditions that agitate the heart. So it would seem useless if a child should then blame his parents, even though they really were the source of his faults.

9. There may be parents who earnestly try to perfect the way they behave, in the hope that later on their children will be of exceptionally good character or fully prepared for life; but their hopes cannot be fulfilled, because their efforts are wrongly directed.

10. So it is better not to take such ways, especially if they only involve strengthening and concentrating the will in order to create something they need, for the results obtained are nothing but fantasies born of the heart.

11. Thus what parents need above all is to be conscious in some degree of the *kejiwaan*, so that they do not later become a target for reproaches from their offspring.

12. For the child it is better not to dwell on this matter, for that only muddles the feelings more, and so makes any later achievements more remote, especially when the aim is to perfect one's life.

13. You, my children, have been fortunate in your life, because you have found a way that is able to rouse the *jiwa*, so that it awakens and can act according to your capacity and the strength that is in you. Little by little your *jiwa* will grow stronger and will eventually be able to fulfil your needs.

14. For that reason, do always practise your *latihan*, so that you may soon encounter the various powers that have gathered in your feelings and be able to tell one from another.

15. For this, you need to realize how these powers behave, so that their way of working may be regulated; this will eventually lead them to work together – that is, to help one another.

16. It is well to remember not to give way to your heart's pressing desire at times to understand the impossible, and especially not to think about the realm of the Great Life. For that is not a subject for thought, and in truth the time for you to reach an understanding of it is still very far off. Moreover, if your mind does this, it will not enable you to achieve your hopes more quickly; on the contrary, if your mind is not strong enough, it may become very agitated.

17. So it is best to do your training patiently, even though you make progress in it only little by little. The main thing for you is to experience its truth, so that you may develop in the best way.

18. Besides that, those who are undertaking this training must also be reminded here never to neglect their obligations – for example, not to reject the ordinary life of people on earth. On the contrary, it is hoped they will provide the world with all the arts and skills useful to society. To do that is truly a task set for mankind by the Will of God.

19. It must be remembered too that mankind has been created to inhabit the earth, and that the earth exists to provide for human needs. So if someone deliberately isolates himself and ignores the activity of his physical faculties – paying no attention to sights, sounds, smells, feelings, and so on – then in truth he is acting contrary to the Will of God, because he is wasting what God has given him.

20. So you must not behave like that. The best and most fitting way to live is that you should work to meet the needs of your existence by bringing the feelings throughout your body to life, so that every part of it feels responsible for your role as a human being, whose specialised parts together form a unity.

21.   That way is best and really fitting for the life of a noble creature, and it also enables him to fulfil his commitment to put his life in order and meet its every need, both inner and outer. So, my children, behaviour which leads you astray should rightly be avoided, for it can make your high qualities vanish and the glory be lost from the excellent instruments or faculties that take part in your life.

22.   That is why it is best for all of you to let these human instruments make a stand against the influence of the powers that always interfere in your feelings, to stop these powers impeding your progress in life and to let them instead become of themselves really useful aides to you.

23.   Now to discuss the existence of powers connected with human life. The first, or rather the lowest, is the power of matter. This force is situated of course in objects that evidently cannot move by themselves.

24.   These things, although evidently unable to move of their own accord, nevertheless contain power of the same kind as that in man's mind; hence people can make use of these things for a range of tasks and can also shape and colour them as they wish.

25.   Because of the mutual attraction between the material force and man's mind, people have finally become able to make a variety of objects that can meet their every need.

26.   So, in short, people have been able to create all kinds of devices which they can use for their adornment, shelter or dwelling, for their household needs, for travelling, for agriculture, and so on.

27.   In sum, because man wants a way of life that lacks nothing he is obliged to create such accessories.

28.   He must therefore be able to use them rightly, so that he may bring order and well-being into the general life of his kind.

29.   Such is the reality man must truly be aware of, to prevent the reverse from happening, with man becoming the tool of his own tools for living.

30.   So much about matter, which seems powerless but which actually exerts a strong attraction, because in reality it has an affinity with the human mind.

2

DHANDHANGGULA

1. From what has been said above, it would seem that a person could repel the influence of the material force with ease. In fact it is not so. For although material objects have been created and fashioned by man, their power of attraction has in truth so affected his mind and penetrated his feelings that, if cut off from his possessions, he often feels as though deprived of half his soul.

2. Really, if one remembers that all these things owe their existence to man, it certainly seems beyond belief that they should have so much power over him. Yet it is precisely because they are creations of his heart and mind and energy that they do exert this attraction on human feelings. Many people even reverse the normal state of affairs and, instead of making use of things as ordinary products, regard them as objects to worship, able to bestow blessings on them. And there are also other people altogether incapable of using their possessions according to need, but who on the contrary are completely ruled and used by them.

3. That is why many rich people, just because of their wealth, look on others not so rich as themselves as inferior. This is caused solely by the influence of the material force which has been absorbed into their feelings.

4. This leads also to tensions and conflicts between rich and poor. True, the two associate at times, but that is because the labour of the poor is needed for the pursuit of profits, not through feelings of love and brotherhood.

5. So they just part company when the labour of the poor is no longer required. Thus whether their association will last or not depends entirely on the influence of the power of matter.

6.   Rightly understood, however, wealth or material things are simply and solely aids needed for organizing human society in the best way, so as to bring order and prosperity to society.

7.   Men do indeed need material objects as aids, and everyone has to have them. The more a man has and the greater their variety, the better. But it has to be remembered that he must be aware of their use and how to manage them; he must not let them become objects of worship.

8.   It is to be hoped also that a man will not be influenced by material things; on the contrary, he has to be able to control them. The way for you to realize this is by doing your *latihan* patiently and sincerely. For from the training will come evidence, little by little, of how the material force works in your feelings, so that you may channel it in its rightful direction. This awareness will then lead at length to your self and the material force working in co-operation – though with different duties – so that you will not need to discard or avoid possessions.

9.   Now to go on to how the material force of other things influences a man – a sharp weapon for example. Rightly, this is only a means to repel approaching danger, not in the least an instrument for killing people. But when the possessor of such a weapon is heedless or incautious the influence of its force, transforming his feelings, is truly dangerous for him. For it makes him feel very strong and more than naturally powerful, with the result that he is ready to use his weapon not to ward off approaching danger but against anybody he wants to overpower or master.

10.   Such is the effect of the material power of weapons on a man who is so incautious or heedless that, whether he wishes it or not, his feelings are in fact channelled or carried over into the insensible realm of matter. And further, such a man habitually enjoys quarrelling with other people even though they are not his enemies.

11. Such behaviour will certainly cause disappointment to his fellows, and the feelings of love and brotherhood between them and him will vanish. This, too, is a result of the influence of the power of matter on anybody who is not firmly established as a creature of high level.

12. Even so, because he still has a human nature, he will still have a chance to improve his condition if he finds a way that can train him to reach his inner self. The pressure of the material force on him will then grow weaker and weaker with the strengthening of his human *jiwa*, which can then correct his bad habits.

13. That, my children, is just to show how the power of matter sways the human self. Those material objects, seemingly lifeless and owing their existence to man, really contain a living essence that can influence and be influenced by other forces and even human feelings.

14. So people must heed this, especially those who feel that their mind and *jiwa* are weak. Furthermore, they should make themselves willing to mix with or draw near to people who they hope may be able to guide them towards the *kejiwaan*, where they will really obtain evidence enabling them to feel the difference among the forces that have gathered in their feelings, and to know which are from themselves, which are material and other ancillary forces, and which are from the One who keeps watch.

15. So is it if you earnestly wish for this and are able to attain it. You really do need to remember that although man has noble and excellent qualities, fully equipping him for life, unless he is aware of his nobility and understands how to use his qualities, his very nobility and endowment for living will themselves cause him suffering. To avoid this, he needs to begin the training of the self, and if he is fortunate he will later get the clear guidance referred to above.

16. You and all those following the training will, it is now hoped, heed what has been said. Human nature, fully fitted for living as it is, has a wide-ranging life and activities, so that all kinds of forces enter it. This can be compared with sugar and its sweetness. For they cannot be separated from each other nor can one rid itself of the other; on the contrary, the two have to co-operate – that is to say, the noble one, man, must be able to channel the flow of forces to where they are required, and for his own benefit he must fulfil his duties and obligations without harming the interests of other forces. This is how difficult it is, my children, so may you not do your *latihan* less because you feel you are already trained and can receive the whisper of the *jiwa* as well as make a variety of movements and freely utter sounds.

17. Since you have begun to develop only recently, you still need to feel accurately the sources of what you receive, so that later you will recognize what the reality is. So, my children, you must not hastily feel satisfied or be proud because you have become a link for those interested in this way of training people.

18. Never imagine, my children, especially with regard to that last point, that you have already reached the goal, for your state spiritually is still an ordinary one. Do realize that anybody who has also undergone this training, especially anybody who has experienced the *latihan kejiwaan* for some time, is filled in some measure with the strength of the life force, which encompasses him both within and without, particularly at moments when he is empty of thought. If at just such times he is near other people who earnestly wish for this training, these people will soon spontaneously feel a vibration, and some of them may then make movements. There is no need to enlarge on this, because you have all had this experience the first time you received.

19. Really this condition is an ordinary one in the realm of the *jiwa*, but the person who is the link (the opener) probably deserves to be commended, because at that moment he will at least experience the unpleasantness of the suffering in feelings released from the body of the person being opened, while the latter, on the contrary, will feel as if relieved of a heavy burden.

20. So you must not be satisfied just with reaching that stage; rather, when standing (as a helper) by a brother who is being opened, do feel what is being received, so that you not only witness what is happening to him but can also receive what you need for your own self.

21. In this state you can make good progress, for it will become apparent how the forces that have gathered in the feelings combine and separate.

22. By this means the suffering that comes to you from helping or opening a new member will no longer be a heavy burden, but will even increase your own smooth progress towards the identity of a human being. Moreover, because you are in this state, the opening will be more satisfactory for the new member you are standing by.

23. Now for the force that is embodied in fine clothes and likewise in radiant, sparkling jewellery. These have no less powerful an influence on people. If their owners' feelings are swayed by them, their behaviour, formerly friendly, will become arrogant, in the sense that they will feel themselves superior, grander, better-looking and more splendid than other people.

24. So much so that the essence of their feelings is really the essential force of the things they own, and, by the very fact of their feelings being filled with the power of matter, these people are of course unaware of it.

25. At times they are ridiculous too, because they are apt to behave in an exaggerated way; but, far from feeling this is wrong, they even think it proper and laudable.

26.   People whose feelings have been deceived by the power of matter go so far astray that they are no longer able to distinguish between what is right and what is wrong, between what in themselves must be master or user and what has to be ruled and used.

27.   Similarly, classes of people in different circumstances from those referred to above are also duped by the effect of the power of matter. Furthermore, many other kinds of material objects whose forces strongly sway the course of people's lives need to be discussed.

28.   Objects of this sort are: harrows, ploughs, scythes, sickles, hoes and other such tools used in agriculture, particularly for work in paddy-fields and on farmland.

29.   Because the peasants use these tools to cultivate their paddy-fields and land, the feelings of those who lack inner strength easily sink into the realm of matter. Consequently many peasants have a narrow outlook on existence, thus limiting their well-being in life to merely where they are.

30.   Consequently, many of them, happening to live in poverty, are compelled to resign themselves and accept their lot – meaning that they are unwilling to make any effort to leave their villages. Some are even frightened if they go out, and some are shy of meeting people who seem prosperous and are good at expressing themselves.

3
KINANTHI

1. So it is clear how, owing to the influence of the force of matter on a person's feelings, those feelings are close to the essence of material objects.

2. Also because of that strong influence, together with the weakness of his will and *jiwa*, he no longer cares to reflect that beyond his immediate surroundings are many places and kinds of work that would offer him a better life.

3. Clearly, then, his so-called patience and acceptance of his lot result simply and solely from the effect of the force contained in his own tools.

4. This is completely the wrong way round, for the man is not, as he should be, able to make use of his tools; instead, the tools govern his whole existence, so that it can be said that his life and death are determined just by them.

5. Indeed, such has his condition become that he scarcely remembers that the world is wide and contains every kind of thing needed for human life.

6. This is also the effect of the kind of force in matter. So perhaps we should not hastily blame or criticize one whose sole satisfaction is in hoeing and work like that, and whose habit is to go to sleep soon after coming back from the fields.

7. And because his feelings have sunk so far down, it does not even occur to him that, if only he discovered it, there is something that could be compared with a lamp within the human self that could guide him to a fitting way to live.

8. Thus if a man remembers, or could remember, that human nature is the nature of a high creature, he ought to be able to understand better and also behave better than creatures of other kinds.

9.   A man must also be able to broaden his outlook on life so that he can pave or select the way to well-being.

10.   Then he will certainly be able to achieve his wish in life: to ensure the welfare of his family and later be taken as an example by his descendants.

11.   Do not, therefore, be so easily swayed by the power of material things that you feel satisfied with a mouthful of rice. And do not always be so ready to speak of patience and resignation, as if circumstances were inevitable and decreed by God.

12.   Such remarks are out of place. They come mainly from facile talk which, as yet, is without understanding of the true meaning of fate.

13.   Talk like that, moreover, is truly a curse on your own self and will most likely affect your innocent descendants.

14.   Such is the danger when a person is ignorant about the truth of the self, for it may be said he is compelled to swallow the influence of the power of matter, whatever it may be.

15.   Truly tragic though this is when perceived, a man cannot be blamed for it, because his feelings have not come under the sway of the material force by his own wish. So strong is the effect of that force on the human self, in fact, that a man may often appear as though he wilfully prefers misery and poverty to the effort of seeking a way to a happier life.

16.   So far below his human status may he fall when his feelings have been influenced by the force of matter. Therefore you should quickly make an effort to seek true guidance that can train the self to become aware of how the material force works in the feelings.

17.   Having done this, you will be able to discover also what is the sort of work that it is your natural right to do, or what path you need to take.

18. Of course this cannot be achieved all at once, but in the *latihan* you will gradually receive indications until the moment when it only remains for you to choose the job to do.

19. By doing your right work, it will happen of itself that your worship of God – required of you as a human being by your inner self – will not lessen. Truly this is the best way, for people do not then work solely for worldly purposes, and worshipping God as well cannot be abandoned.

20. By doing what has been described, you will truly experience peace and happiness, not only in your life in this world but in the hereafter also.

21. Now to discuss another kind of object: namely, goods dealt in by traders in markets, shops and other places.

22. These goods have an effect just as terrible on the people who deal in them, if their *jiwa* is weak.

23. The influence of the power in these goods goes even deeper because they are continually coming and going, always bringing a profit or causing a loss. Hence the feelings of the traders are all the more affected by the force in the goods they buy and sell, and so sink ever deeper into the realm of matter.

24. On the face of it, however, this is not to be regretted, for this is indeed how traders look for profit; and the profit they gain is then used to supply the necessities of life for their families.

25. The energetic ones work very hard in the pursuit of profit, in order to become rich quickly, heedless at times of physical fatigue.

26. The important thing to traders is to think of ways to make their buying and selling profitable. Thus in many instances their feelings contain nothing but the images of the goods they deal in.

27.   Apparently this is no problem to traders, but a necessity rather, to enable them to calculate accurately, in order that their dealings may be sure to yield a good profit.

28.   Such is the condition of traders, so that they often set aside other needs not connected with their business, as if unconcerned even to have time to be quiet.

29.   This kind of existence has probably become a necessity for traders, for otherwise they certainly would not be and could not be traders in the true sense of the word.

30.   So they cannot be blamed for their ways; nor is the use of their minds for this purpose to be deplored, since people still have to use their minds, if only a little, even for the most ordinary work.

31.   This also can be justified, for the mind is in fact a means to enable men to think out everything that needs to be done or arranged. Even so, men must also use their mental ability to enable them to become aware of their inner self, and so understand that the master of their life is not the mind but the *jiwa,* the human inner force.

32.   For the traders, however, it will not be easy to do what has just been said, for they are already under the spell of the force of the goods they are always thinking about. Moreover, because they think so much about the goods they deal in, their characters unsuspectedly but automatically change and become like the force in those goods.

33.   So a trader's mind, when completely subject to the force of the goods that fill his thoughts, is no longer calm, and he will have difficulty in quietening himself if he needs to do so later in order to possess his true identity.

34.   Further, his mind gets so far carried away that it gives no more thought whatever to his inner self, but keeps darting here and there like money that is always changing hands, so that his life resembles a piece of flotsam tossing up and down in mid-ocean.

35. So, clearly, human beings who want to possess their inner self may not just follow every impulse of their minds, but must also empty their minds by quietening the self. This is in order that they may experience a state quite beyond expectation; and it is precisely this state that will truly guide them to a life of well-being.

36. The inner feeling of a man who is aware of the *kejiwaan*, even if he does the usual work of a trader, will not easily be swayed by the force of the wares he deals in. Rather, all the mental activity connected with his goods can be supervised by his inner self.

37. That is the ideal and, being human, a man ought to be able to act in that manner, for by so doing his life will prosper and he will be able to arrange it rightly – meaning that in all his work he will spontaneously maintain his worship of God Almighty.

38. Such is the right way for a man already aware of his real being. So, though externally doing all sorts of work, using his mind to the full, he is aware of the border between the mind and the inner self. It is another matter for people interested only in material things.

39. The more so if their interests are really profitable. They will then work even harder in pursuit of still bigger profits.

40. Because of their delight that all their undertakings make profits, their love of material possessions goes ever more deeply into them, until they love these possessions more than they love their families and close friends.

41. Some go so far that love of possessions even exceeds their love and affection for their children, so that hostility often arises between father and son over material things.

42. This applies especially to those who are always successful, who profit from everything they undertake. If they neglect their inner self, they will fall into the abyss of the material world.

43. In general, the nature of traders – specifically of those who think only material things important – is never to feel satisfied, even though they have become rich, and in fact they recognize no limit.

44. Such is the effect of the power in material objects. Be aware, then, that the power in these objects can so influence a man that his mind loses its vision and no longer believes in the life after death.

45. Clearly, then, the effect of the material force is very damaging to human beings who need to become conscious of their *jiwa*. The point is the same as was made earlier – that their characters will change and become like the nature of the force in material objects, which knows nothing of the inner life.

46. No wonder, then, that there are traders who completely forget the needs of their *jiwa*. Every day they think only of their possessions and of ways to make the utmost profit, despite the stress and strain of the work.

47. It is still more disastrous if a person comes so to worship his possessions that they are regarded as if they were the master of his life.

48. The result is that the being of man, a sublime creature of God, has fallen lower in the order of eternal life than the level of those material objects. So these failings have disjoined the lives of the rich and the poor. The rich even look on the poor as objects of no value.

49. Some wealthy people even take pleasure in toying with the lives of the poor as though they were inanimate things. They lure the poor into maintaining their wealth, so that these needy ones do not realize that, in fact, they are being used as a means for the pursuit of the biggest possible profit.

50.   Not understanding this, and also being easily led, the poor, in carrying out the duties they have undertaken in return for promises made to them, uphold the interests of the rich as zealously as they would uphold their own. Hence, when successful in this charge they feel as proud as if they had achieved a splendid triumph.

51.   In fact, though, as already explained, they are influenced only by the material force, which has deceived their feelings because of their heedlessness. So they are forever unhappy, even in the life after death.

52.   Behaviour of this kind indeed greatly damages a person's life. A man must not be willing to become the slave of the material force. On the contrary, as a human being he should be able to master it, not be mastered by it and have the relationship reversed, as happens to people who lack a firm wish to discover the wisdom of the realm of the *jiwa*.

53.   This therefore is best for you: even though you work as a trader, it is to be hoped that you will not neglect to keep watch over your inner self. Do be really careful in all your behaviour, and see your condition as it actually is.

54.   Only, you must not be mistaken about this, for this state is not something ordinary that can easily be seen as one sees with the eyes in the usual way. It is something that arises in, and always accompanies, the course of thinking. So you need to be alert to enable you to know within your knowing.

55.   This is difficult for anyone whose self has had no training yet, but you who have been able to do the *latihan* can feel and be aware of your condition. To be able to understand this, it is best to be trained in the following way:

56.   When you are looking, feel and see the different kinds of seeing. When you are listening, feel and listen to the

different kinds of hearing. When you are smelling, feel and smell the different kinds of smelling, and while speaking feel the different kinds of speaking.

57. Likewise, do always be aware of your entire body – of what you feel and the nature of the changes it undergoes each time you encounter anything. This is the first step, a beginning for you in getting evidence of how one force differs from another; later you will be able to feel which impulse comes from which one of these forces that are always active together and that in reality contribute to everything you do.

58. This is the way to receive, even though you do it amid the turmoil of life. So, not surprisingly, some people choose another way: that is, by removing themselves far from the turmoil. This is not the right solution, however, because wherever a man may go he cannot leave his thinking behind, and it is precisely this that always interferes with his actions.

59. Probably you will no longer find it difficult to receive everything that has been mentioned. Only, there is still a lack within you: you are still unable to do it thoroughly.

60. May you not worry about that. Just keep on, even though the results come only little by little. In the end the time will certainly come when whatever is needed will become clear spontaneously – provided that in your inner feeling you do not go on stressing the importance of your thinking, for that truly is the main source of temptation on your way towards your eternal self.

4
PANGKUR

1. While receiving, it is best to put your thinking aside, in order to let the feeling in your body be pure and clear. For truly the mind always hampers progress in receiving, and indeed by nature it enjoys thinking about matters that make no sense and imagining things that overstep the bounds of reality.

2. Now to tell of something else: that is, of the things that comprise the instruments and the other requirements for writing, and also about the nature of the mental skills learned in schools or centres of study.

3. All these also embody the pull or power of the material force. Plainly, then, brainworkers from clerks to high-ranking officials use skills in their work that are derived from the force of matter.

4. That being so, both a person's thoughts and the work thought about and done are encompassed by the material force.

5. He certainly does not guess, and possibly would not believe, that material objects could sway his thinking to such an extent, seeing that these things are made by man; yet this is the very reason why people do not realize that their heart and mind are activated by the power of matter.

6. The greater part of mankind does not yet suspect this, for the instrument needed to understand and analyse the differences and the division of the forces remains of such a nature that people cannot truly feel which of the contents of their heart and mind come from man's inner self and which from matter. This is why one must not always trust the heart and mind and follow their will. In other words, though people should not forsake their heart and mind, they must be able to recognize the sources of the impulses which finally shape their will.

7.   This being the case, please do not misunderstand what has just been said and deliberately negate the zeal of the heart and mind, thus weakening your efforts to live a life of the best kind here on earth. The root of the problem is this, that you need to understand the differences in kind between the forces associated with your life and the force of man's inner self. Once these forces have been put into order, people will be able to conduct their lives as befits human beings called noble creatures.

8.   There is nothing wrong in having a well-developed mind. On the contrary, as many people as possible need to acquire advanced and wide-ranging knowledge, provided such knowledge really becomes a means for them to live as God ordains and a means to better the lives of their fellow men. Doing this will enable them to reach the level of creatures who can broaden the scope of their life to benefit society.

9.   That is the use of men of ability, so that with their knowledge they may fill the world with all the arts and skills helpful to human society, and that the light of these, shining radiantly, may enable society to live in peace and prosperity.

10.   So will it be, my children, when the role of knowledge is understood. Thus there is truly nothing wrong in people seeking knowledge. Rather is it a need, a necessity, for it enables them to lead fuller lives. The case can be likened to that of a master and servant: it is all right to have a stupid servant, but still better to have a clever one. Only, it is necessary to remember that the master must not then let himself be made a fool of by his servant.

11.   So the master must be aware to what extent his servant (the heart and mind) is clever. And he must also know what the habits of this servant are. For unless he understands his

servant's cleverness, the master can easily be fooled by it and will inevitably sink into a trough of misery.

12. For this reason, many people, at the end of their life's journey, regret the outcome of their actions. The cause is solely their own misdeeds, for they simply followed the impulses of the heart and mind without knowing their source, and were unaware that they came from a force other than their human inner self.

13. These people then blame themselves and even their families, feeling that their families too have partly caused their errors. Such is the attitude of those who do not understand about man's nobility and so do not feel the guidance for their life that is present in their *jiwa*.

14. It is different for one who has discovered the true meaning of man's noble status. The nature of feelings that arise in the body and how the heart and mind work with their associated forces will be made clear to him, and hence he will prosper and be happy in everything he does.

15. This is the best path to enable him to live in the state he hopes for. Nevertheless many people still give this matter no attention. Indeed, those who happen to live in luxury and have highly developed minds may have only the faintest feeling for the subject of the inner self. Because the right way is still unknown to them as yet, their attention is always on the extent and importance of the material force.

16. As time goes on, their outlook on life and their mental interests focus more and more on the material world, until they reach a state of mind in which their life is like a coconut shell in mid-ocean, tossed to and fro by the waves. Inevitably, then, the life and death of such people can be said to be at the mercy of the power of matter.

17. Such is the kind of influence exerted by the power of matter. So, not surprisingly, there are people whose conduct goes beyond the limits or whose deeds deviate from what is fitting. For these people are not clever at making use of their cleverness, but on the contrary are used by it. So in reality they are victimized by their own ability.

18.   That is as seen from the viewpoint of man's inner self, but the people who behave in this way do not believe they are in the least at fault. Rather, they sometimes regard their clearly wrong behaviour as a mark of importance and superiority. When accused of something, they even go so far as to put the blame on their accusers, even at times confirming their counter-charges under oath.

19.   Thus does the power of matter triumph over people still weak in their inner self. For, as explained earlier, the material force can get into people's thought and imagination. Hence, my children, do realize that you must be able to see the different forces contained in everything you do, so that you may find a fitting path for your life.

20.   By this means your condition will be a balanced one, in which the activity of the inner self will always be followed by the heart and mind, and they will only do the duties given them. So it will be as when there is a master who gives orders and a servant who carries out the tasks he is told to do. In such circumstances a sharp mind will be more useful than a dull one.

21.   The outcome, when you can behave in that way, will be that at length you will find peace in your life and while working at your daily tasks will always remember the Greatness of God.

22.   This means that whenever you are working you will be accompanied spontaneously by praise of the Greatness of God, and hence in whatever you do you will get the guidance you need. Such is the bliss of those who have been granted the Grace of God, and through it they will be more obedient in all things to God's Power.

23.   Now to come to the less educated people, who generally have jobs only as clerks and the like, and who work for their living merely because the needs of life compel them to.

24.   If they have not yet had guidance from the inner self, their inner feeling will be in greater darkness, for they feel that the locality where they work is the only place to live and they no longer give a thought to other places where they could also make a living.

25.   So they feel no urge to change their location, particularly if their employer takes notice of them and if their pay is often raised. These things strengthen their loyalty to their employers and make them feel sure that the place where they work is the place for them to live their lives out.

26.   Such is the state of mind of people really under the sway of the material force. Their *jiwa* not being revived yet, naturally they cannot feel inner guidance about a suitable course for their life, and their minds are no longer open to accept advice and explanations from other people about a better and broader path of life which could ensure their permanent security.

27.   The cause of their attitude is that they have been put in thrall by the power of matter. If at length they meet with hardship through dismissal from their work, only then do they realize that the job was not of a kind to which they could cling forever.

28.   Consequently, in time, they feel benighted and so see no sign of the broad prospects that lie beyond the scope of their ability to think. This state forces them to abase their inner feeling and be ready to enslave themselves to anybody who may be able to give them some measure of security.

29.   Some security seems indispensable to people misled all their life by the power of matter. They therefore have no inkling that, in truth, their self is always accompanied by guidance for the course of their life.

30.   This guidance, which certainly is present within one, is truly something that comes easily – more easily than thinking about anything, for it appears when the activity of the mind is stilled. Yet, easily though it comes, a man cannot readily stop the mind's activity, because it has been so very strongly influenced by the power of matter. This problem can be tackled before hardship is experienced, but many people, while still living in comfort, feel that they have no time to examine their inner self. Having long come under the power of matter, they are more interested in the path of materialism.

5

MEGATRUH

1. Consequently their inner feeling diverges ever more from their real being, so that they fall into darkness and their mind is adept only at picturing things that can never be put into effect.

2. At times they show a desire to work for a living, but this is due solely to pressure by friends or other people. At times too they feel impelled to do a dishonest job.

3. Such a state of affairs has even become commonplace among people of limited understanding, for it exactly matches their mind which, filled with the material force, knows not the pattern of the perfect life.

4. Certainly, my children, as leading creatures you must strengthen the bond between your inner feeling and the One who watches over you, so that you may readily obtain all that you truly need. And doing that will signify that you really are high creatures of God.

5. Thus you will no longer be just things filled with air, but human vessels containing an eternal inner self. So, may you not neglect your training in the realm of the *jiwa*.

6. Nor may you go on being led by your heart and mind, occupied as they are by the *nafsu*, which care only to have what they think will please them, and regard the *kejiwaan* as boring.

7. Whereas the *kejiwaan* must truly be regarded as a necessity – even indeed the main necessity – for your life to be happy.

8. So if you become a clerk, do not at once feel content with what you happen to earn, nor count on your job being permanent, but try to find something real within you that will enable you, when later you meet difficulties, to keep them in perspective.

9. As has been said, your circumstances really cannot be relied on. They very easily change, and indeed always will change. The danger is that these changes are bound to affect you, causing you misfortunes not easy to bear.

10. You should remember that nothing stays as it is. Even something as large as a mountain is sure to change, though man cannot tell when it will change or collapse.

11. It is more alarming still if people entrust their fate just to a small, weak undertaking. It may collapse or change at any time. Sometimes just a drop in profits makes it necessary to reduce the staff.

12. Therefore it is essential for you, without delay, to seek a way to attain insight into life, so that you will be prepared for whatever befalls you.

13. If you can do this, your life will really be happy, and whenever you meet difficulties your inner feeling will not easily be shaken.

14. For you will soon get spontaneous guidance about various jobs you can then do, because you will have had this training and have received indications of the way of working that is best for you and that matches your *jiwa*.

15. Moreover, doing work suitable to the *jiwa* broadens your view of life and your understanding of how to put human life to use, and strengthens the bond with the One who watches over you.

16. If you have achieved this, even though your fellow men do not count you as well-educated, you will not lag far behind in position.

17. Having been trained in the manner spoken of, you will receive whatever guidance you need.

18. Accurately felt, the understanding about the course of your life that comes from the *latihan* is far fuller than you learn at an ordinary place of study. What is more important, you will then no longer enjoy empty chatter and unseemly showing-off.

19. Truly, your own heart and mind will be amazed at how you are able to understand whatever is necessary for your life by a means so simple.

20. This certainly is something extraordinary, beyond expectation; for understanding usually comes from hard mental study, but in this case it is obtained without even making any use of thought.

21. How necessary this is for people who outwardly still know very little, to enable them to get what they so much need! Do not let your self remain in darkness, unable in the least degree to understand your value as a high creature.

22. Such is the importance for man of this *kejiwaan* training. Anyone who does not want to undertake it – especially if his mind is not well-developed – is bound to have endless bitter experiences in his life. The more so when it is remembered that such a man has a weak nature which can always be affected by hazards and dangers.

23. Inescapably, then, he will suffer during his life, and if this suffering goes on and on he is sure also to come to an untimely end.

24. Indeed this often happens. But most people do not think so far ahead. On the contrary, while their labour is still needed by their employers – meaning while they are still needed as tools for the pursuit of profit – they believe they are held in high regard.

25. And among them are some who, being highly regarded by their employers, feel they have authority in their section of the work and then behave arrogantly towards their co-workers.

26.   In these circumstances they very easily become possessed by their work, leaving their heart and mind with no time any more to consider their real self.

27.   Day and night they think of nothing else but their work, until their inner life is similarly affected and is also aware of nothing but their work.

28.   The result of their having lived outwardly and inwardly for their work is, in truth, that later, when death ends their life, their faith will quit them to turn back to that work.

29.   As to matter, if you really fathom its condition you will be able to know that it seems there like our world and also that the beings there resemble mankind in their earnest devotion to God Almighty.

30.   Those entities seem in our world just lifeless things, because in the scheme of human life they are merely tools or aids for mankind's activities; hence human eyes see them merely as things to be made into whatever man wishes.

31.   Nevertheless the life of material things in their own world can be likened to that of a man in his; so things can also worship God at their own level.

32.   Their attitude to God is no different from man's, except that their level or status as creatures of God is far below the human level.

33.   For this reason, material things yearn to be linked to human thought, to enable them to raise their own status to the high level of mankind.

34.   So they unreservedly obey man's will, simply going along with his wishes, in order that they may remain settled close to his mind until the moment he dies.

35.   Material things can thus follow man into his world – a world far higher than that of matter, which in men's eyes seems completely void.

36. That is how life is ordered for matter; and people need to understand it so that they may know the nature of the influence of the material force, which always takes part in their life. Then they will be able to regulate that ancillary force rightly.

37. The truth is that these material things naturally want to join in human activities, for they thus fulfil their destiny – to become the servants of mankind.

38. What happens, however, is the opposite: man serves material things, so instead of raising their level he sinks into the realm of matter.

39. There – could he retain his memory – he would be shocked, because he would be unable to find anything real.

40. He would also feel that nothing he experienced there, in the material realm, tallied at all with his experiences when he was still in the ordinary world.

41. But, my children, the feelings of a man who sinks into the material realm do not remain valid. For once he has gone down into such a realm he is completely immersed in it and therefore no longer has the human feelings he had in the world.

42. In consequence, though he knew it once, he can no longer feel the difference between right and wrong. That place so moulds him that whatever he experiences there feels normal.

43. There, too, are to be found all kinds of pleasure and places of entertainment – in short, many ways to find enjoyment and to display the luxury of his circumstances. On the other hand, suffering is not lacking either.

44. Matter regards this all as a good repayment, for matter is under an obligation to man. So there is no deception in this nor any intention to lead him astray; for matter, this is really an act of true devotion.

45. For the man, however, when it is remembered that mankind's place in the scheme of life is really a sublime one, such a state is worse than wrong. It is a great fault in the man, for he completely fails to live up to his commitment as a creature capable of bringing order to existence.

46. Because such errors are possible, my children, may you never neglect to do reverence to God. Make time for your *latihan,* and never give way to your heart and mind when they suggest that you have no opportunity to do this training any more.

47. If you obey your heart and mind, never in your life will you find time to spare for your necessary worship of God, for the heart and mind are always concerning themselves with matters that lack reality.

48. This is precisely the condition that you must overcome, so that your thoughts will no longer obstruct the self.

49. Moreover, when they have ceased to be obstacles – that is to say, when your heart and mind no longer impede your *latihan* – your actions will be more resolute and mature, and your heart and mind will truly be the self's servant or bondsman.

50. And after that you will soon become aware of and be closely connected with the One who watches over you.

6

ASMARANDANA

1. And when you are in that state indications and counsel of great benefit to your self will pour into you.

2. That, my children, is the good fortune man has been able to receive. Limited though your ordinary mental ability may be, you can yet come to understand all that is necessary without having to use your acquisitiveness, but just by being patient and quiet.

3. You will also become aware of all your past errors and spontaneously repent of what you have done wrong. And it will gladden your heart and make you feel happy that you have really drawn close to the One who watches over you.

4. That is all as to the significance of the power of matter. Now the subject changes to the power of plant-life or vegetation, a force which also takes part in man's life on earth.

5. The power in plants can influence human life even more, for without it man would have no vigour nor a body like his present earthly one.

6. In fact the force from plants is an absolute need for life. From the start, while still in his mother's womb, a human being obtains the essences of plants through his mother, and is thus inseparable from food up to the moment of his birth.

7. God has willed that human strength should come from food derived from plants, so the human body is nourished and formed by plant essences.

8. In short, people certainly cannot do without such food, even though their full diet also includes meat – but that subject is better left until later, after the nature of the force in vegetation has been discussed.

9. The reason for this is to avoid a tangle of subjects that would make it difficult to understand what is really intended.

10. You must realize that actually the essences of the power in plant-life are already present in mankind, though in a form that cannot be detected by the ordinary eyes, but only by an inner feeling that is truly pure – clean and clear or quite free from the influence of thinking. So when the essences of food from plants enter man's body, to form, nourish and strengthen it, their entry signifies a meeting with the essences already there.

11. Truly, then, this is a meeting between external and internal, as between the outer life and the inner. So if what comes from outside is not suited to what is inside, an unpleasant feeling will arise that will readily make the human body unwell.

12. Although flavour cannot be detected by the eyes, the essences of it present in mankind can recognize it by such tastes as sweet, nutty, bitter, sour, hotly spiced, salty, tart and brackish. Mankind is endowed with these essences of flavour, which correspond to the tastes of the food he eats.

13. Foods vary widely in outward form, but are merely vessels for their essences, whose differences lie in taste, the real purpose of which is to make it easy for what is outside and what is inside to meet.

14. And their meeting takes place in man when he eats, which means that, in reality, man when eating is only a medium for the force of the plant essences outside him to meet the force of those within him.

15. The human being who enacts that role has carried out his obligation in this matter properly, and may truly be called a high and enlightened creature of God.

16.   The wisdom of such a person is rightly praised by the participants – that is, the essences, both from inside and from outside, of the power in plant-life – because he has been able, after they have long awaited his help, to open the path to bliss for them.

17.   This meeting between the forces of plant-life from without and within is like a long-awaited meeting between husband and wife. How great is their joy needs no description, for you can imagine it. What does need to be said about this, however, is that in this situation man is already free from the sway of the power of vegetation.

18.   For accomplishing this will enable you to know how life is arranged in the plant world, and also how the influence of its force on mankind can be dangerous, even though all these forces are intended to take part in your life as a creature of high level.

19.   In their outer nature, as food, plants when eaten are of course able to build up the strength of the human body, with its flesh, blood, and so on.

20.   Even so, you should certainly not depend solely on the strength derived from plant-life, for it is really not permitted, as that is only one of the means willed by God to enable you to live on earth.

21.   Thus, had God decreed that mankind be provisioned only with the vital essences of air and water, people would of course be able to live just by breathing air and drinking water. But then they would certainly not have been formed as you are.

22.   Clearly then, as has been said, human beings have to eat grown food because they have been endowed by the Will of God with the essential qualities of such food, in order that eventually these essences should all live together in harmony.

23. Although human food is derived from living plants, when these are eaten or made into food they certainly appear dead.

24. Nevertheless their essences remain alive and await the fulfilment of their desire, spoken of already.

25. Their desire is the same as man's: to find the right way to live in order that, when their end comes, they may return to the glory of the eternal world.

26. So if you do not reach your real level – meaning the level at which you can put your ancillary forces in their right places – naturally you will not be able to rise higher; that is, to the greater, noble life meant for humanity.

27. So is it for plants. Really and truly they long to be united by human agency with their counterparts, and thus return to a high and glorious realm.

28. Hence plants believe it far better for their essences to be eaten by human beings than just to drop to the ground and rot or only become food for animals.

29. Indeed, when eaten by human beings, plants rejoice and greatly praise God and liberally thank mankind for so glorious a death.

30. So their situation, my children, is like that of the force in material objects, discussed earlier. The difference between the two forces is that the material force affects only thinking, whereas the force of plant essences affects the feeling throughout man's body.

31. But although both these forces have so close a link with man, and blend with him, they are only his ancillaries.

32. Now, having completed the explanation of how the force of vegetation acts on mankind, it is best to follow this up without delay by analysing some plants one by one. This is necessary in order that their condition may be more fully understood.

33.   Take first, as an example, the characteristics of the food called rice. Coming from plants grown in paddy fields, it is the staple food – an everyday necessity – for many people.

34.   Paddy is a plant which grows in fields filled with water, and it needs a great amount of water to thrive. Its stalk is slender but fairly long and, besides being hollow, is jointed. It is short-lived, for it ripens fast.

35.   Since paddy needs first and foremost a lot of water, people who eat food derived from it do not withstand suffering well, want only quick satisfactions and a sufficiency for their life, and lack the spirit to exert themselves to raise their standard of living.

36.   Further, their opinions waver, and they have no wish to try to broaden their outlook on life.

37.   Rather, if help does not come their way in life, their feeling is just to put up with things and be left to their lot, simply accepting it, lowly and wretched though their circumstances may be.

38.   The long slim stalk of the rice plant is like a sign that these people, besides feeling insecure, will always have a sense of futility in whatever steps they take, so their hearts will easily become weak-willed and narrow.

39.   The hollow and jointed nature of the stalk means that rice-eaters are emotionally very simple and are apt to let other people know whatever is occupying their hearts, and that their will is disjointed, so they are always undecided about what they want.

40.   The short life and quick maturing of paddy indicate that rice-eaters cannot long sustain their will and are readily satisfied with whatever they get.

41.   Other kinds of foods are also commonly eaten in villages, such as vegetables; these too are planted and cultivated in paddy-fields, and in fact do not differ much from what has been said of paddy.

42.   The effect of eating this sort of food is to make people feel amiable, peaceful, content to stay where they were born, pleased to live simply and to accept whatever lot befalls them.

43.   Thus, eating such food has so affected people's feelings that they lack the capacity to project those feelings beyond rural life.

44.   Fortunately, villagers can also feed on other fare, such as coconut milk and bamboo shoots (bamboo at a very early stage of its growth), which are used for seasoning and flavouring, and come from the coconut palm and the bamboo cane.

45.   Coconut palms can grow without attention and any-where, even when shut in by other vegetation. Their trunks are big and tall, straight and strong, and branchless. The coconuts grow at the top of the tree, which bears them almost without pause.

46.   So those who eat coconut may have not only the characteristics mentioned above, but also a broad outlook and great self-reliance even in disorganized conditions of life. They may also have firmly rooted opinions not readily swayed by other people, and they are not easily caught by life's temptations.

47.   Further, the position of the fruit and the almost con-tinuous bearing of fruit signify that those who eat it like to store away the fruits of their skill and knowledge, to stop other people having access to them. At times, however, if somebody really wins their confidence, they will share them almost unreservedly.

48.   Other food comes from the bamboo cane, which has a rather slim, long, straight and pliable stem, hollow, divided into sections and covered with prickly hairs that deter anyone who wants to touch it.

49.   This food broadens people's outlook, but in that breadth of view they often feel indecisive, for they lack the strength to stand up to the constant pressure of circumstances.

50.   Fortunately, however, this will not cause a complete breakdown, for they always have the ingenuity and resourcefulness to ward that off.

51.   The hollow, sectional bamboo stem means that, though these people are pleased to be frank and open, again and again this is thwarted because they remain filled with anxiety.

52.   The prickly hairs covering the bamboo stem make these people very much relish provoking quarrels, thus acting as irritants to other people and causing the seeds of conflict between one and another to sprout.

53.   Such are the effects on the human self of the power in plant-life. That is why people are very easily swayed by that force, which can lead to their downfall from their status as principal creatures, who in reality should be the mainstay of all the creatures on earth.

54.   Being so easily swung this way and that by the forces which are his ancillaries in life, man can no longer find the way to fulfil his commitment to become the teacher of all other creatures.

55.   Man must be able to open the way for these forces in him to meet their counterparts and so enable them to live a sublime life after death.

56.   On the face of it, this view cannot possibly be justified, for it is beyond belief that mere plants could have such opinions, since they lack minds and there is nothing to show that they are capable of considering the problems of their life.

57.   That attitude is indeed tenable, being based simply on what the mind knows; but for you, who have to some extent fathomed your own being, a mental view like that is not confirmed by the inner feeling.

58.   So, in fact, if you fail to order your life in the right way you will not escape, and will really feel, the ill effects of this on your life.

59.   In general, then, villagers' feelings vary little from those mentioned. Usually these people are content to give way and just accept whatever befalls them. This sort of attitude is in fact much to be praised if it comes from the inner feeling, but if not – that is to say, if it is merely reaction to the pressure of the forces of plant-life and matter – then this readiness to put up with whatever happens is sure only to lead them astray.

60.   That is why many villagers always live in poor conditions. Easily deceived by shrewder people, they are unable to live free and independent lives, but are subject their whole life long to the will of others who are astute enough to gull them. So however painstakingly they work, they reap little benefit for themselves, the profit falling almost entirely to those who know how to exploit them.

7
DHANDHANGGULA

1. Such is the fate of people who live in villages. Owing to the effect of the force of vegetation, which has become the content of their body and has thus formed in them feelings of the sort mentioned, villagers are easily tempted by people adept at misleading them with pleasing promises. But their promises are only a ruse to entice the villagers, to prevent them seeing what tricks these astute ones are really playing on them.

2. The behaviour of these astute ones looks – especially to the villagers' eyes – like that of true benefactors, and the villagers really feel that they are getting help for their every need, but in fact this help is a chain with which sooner or later they will shackle themselves.

3. They thus go so far that their fate then depends entirely on the astute ones, for whom in reality they come to be merely tools. In other words, they no longer feel free in their work nor have the sense of independence they need in life, so their earthly existence is worthless. That is the harvest for people who have no care for their status as high creatures enveloped by the Power of God Almighty, whereby they could easily receive guidance to enable them to find a suitable way to live.

4. Now about people who live in towns. Speaking generally, they also eat rice and vegetables, but since all kinds of food are available in towns, they eat other foods besides rice and vegetables.

5. Leaving aside meat, town people eat other food from plants, and it is not lacking in variety. In short, people can eat all sorts of food in towns.

6. There is no need, then, to describe in each case the influence that town dwellers have absorbed of the force of these foods derived from plants, but only to give a general idea of the nature of this influence on these people.

7. Owing to the influence of the great assortment of such foods, most town people have such a variety of feelings that occasionally some of these feelings overflow and then flow back and flood their self – in the sense of overwhelming and muddling the working of the mind.

8. This mental muddle makes the people feel that they no longer have a chance to think about their real nature, although in fact this nature – if they had been able to recognize it – could give them enough guidance for them to find, at length, the way of life really fitting for them.

9. Their condition is of course not to be wondered at, for they have become powerless to resist the pressure of all these various forces. In other words, a man whose lot is like that can no longer feel the human force within him. For the feeling designed to enable him to be aware of the human force has long been filled by the various forces that have entered him; so he will not easily regain that feeling unless he meets someone really able to help rid him of all the obstacles within him.

10. Unless he meets such a person, he will go further and further astray, no longer caring to know the true content of his self. Instead, his feelings will become more and more confused, which will greatly intensify his thinking and imagining, and make his body a nest of thoughts and illusions.

11. Some of these people succeed in their efforts to earn enough to live on, and some too make satisfactory profits. As a result, other people usually take these latter as models and immediately imitate them, hoping that their efforts will bring them similarly pleasing profits.

12. Of course, most imitative efforts of this sort cannot yield the results hoped for, since they are not in harmony with these people's inner feeling, not suitable to their self. Rather, if the people do not truly realize their error – that is to say, if they

will not stop trying to imitate other people – then undoubtedly they will come to grief, for they will keep on suffering losses.

13.   And many people work in different ways to make a living. Some work merely because friends urge them to do so, some because they see other people looking very busy at various jobs. Clearly, to work for such reasons is to be the same as a machine, a lifeless thing which only moves if someone sets it in motion. The fact is that these people are still unaware of the significance work has for mankind.

14.   So they work without understanding the limits within which one should work; for instance, they do a job unsuited to the strength of their inner feeling and the capacity of their brain. This is why quite a number of them fall ill, for they put their inner feeling and their brain under stress.

15.   Some of them, too, are jealous of their co-workers, because they themselves do not do so well in their work or because their progress does not get as much attention from their employers, so that quarrels arise between them. Again, not a few businessmen keep suffering losses and then adopt wrong ways of making up those losses.

16.   All this is caused by the various forces which have filled the inner feeling and the mind and made these faculties into tools that serve only the will of the forces raging unchecked within a man's self.

17.   So, in truth, do these forces – the power of matter and the power of vegetation – influence man. This being so, he just has to accept it, which leads to gross neglect of his obligations as a human being and to enjoyment of things that are wrong. Thus his will is no longer that of a human being, but one really and truly usurped by his ancillary forces.

18.   For this reason, my children, let us hope you will not neglect your obligations as human beings. Do your *latihan* in earnest, even though you have long been under the influence of those forces. If you do your *latihan* sincerely,

the influence of these forces will spontaneously separate so that your relationship with them will in fact be like the mixing and separating of water and oil.

19.   When you have reached that level, my children, you will find your self able to understand the true path of your life and also to follow your will which is guided by the Power of God. You can thus come to be aware how the forces referred to and also your own force operate in your inner feeling, so that you may make your human force and your ancillary forces work together.

20.   This really has to be done during your earthly life. Clearly, it should no longer be just a subject for discussion, limited to talk. So, as has just been said, you ought to make a start while still on earth, to avoid anxiety later on about what will happen to you.

21.   Otherwise this subject will only get as far as the mind, supplemented with fine or high-sounding words, and in the end be simply something to talk about.

22.   In those circumstances the truth cannot possibly be understood. This is why the training of the self in the way described above will greatly benefit you, for thereby you will easily be able to receive and understand what needs to be grasped about right and wrong, even in matters that have been much discussed in books.

23.   That will be the outcome of your training, if you do it in earnest. So, may you not neglect your *latihan* nor like to turn it into a subject of meaningless and empty discussion. For such heedlessness will greatly harm your self, causing your feelings to be easily swayed in course of time by fine words which seem true and trustworthy.

24.   Do realize my children, that the insight described above is not very subtle or difficult to attain. In fact, it is easier to attain than to solve problems by means of thinking. Why people find it difficult to attain is that they always use their

mind for this purpose, whereas here thinking has only a supporting part to play. It must never be to the fore, but behind the inner feeling. To make it clear, truth of this nature can be reached only when a person's mind is truly in the wake of the inner feeling, acting only as a follower or subordinate.

25.   This has to be understood in order that in your *latihan* you may always receive guidance that suits your *jiwa*. At length you will be able to know what is true and what is not true in all stories told in books, and hence feel added zeal for the training of your self as well as for doing your daily work.

26.   What is more important is that, when you have reached this level, you will certainly no longer care to take your lead from and put your trust in stories told in fine and high-sounding language. For do realize, my children, that in many of these stories their truth is very far from what is said in them, and that there are also many stories designed to symbolize the course of human life.

27.   Going back to what was said of how the force of vegetation exerts its influence, one would probably never suspect how it could happen that plants and other growing things are just like human beings, able to feel happy or disappointed, and also that many of them feel dislike and even hate for everything they have to face.

28.   So also with the nature of stories: you will be able to know whether their content is true or not, whether the writing really contains truth or is merely a product of the imagination. Do realize, then, that the mind is extremely clever in using language, and so the reader is confused.

29.   Some stories, moreover, because of their excellent literary style, readily move the reader to such a degree that he unhesitatingly declares and believes them true, although in fact most of them are only concerned with beauty of expression and really cannot show any true content. Even so,

this does not call for reproach, for of course it is customary for the heart and mind.

30. Thus it is, my children, so you must not worry about it, even though you live in a town, provided, as has been said, you do not neglect your *latihan*. Then neither of these forces – the force of matter and the force of vegetation – will remain obstacles in your life.

31. Rather, if you can do as advised, and open the way for these forces so that they can easily meet their counterparts, they will serve you in repayment, meaning that food will always come to you; you will never go short of it in your life.

32. Now it is the turn for the significance of the animal force to be explained; that is to say, the characteristics of food derived from the flesh of various animals.

33. The influence of this force in the human body is all the greater and stronger because it goes deeper, and so human energy is almost entirely aroused and activated by the animal force.

34. This being so, it is not beyond belief to a man himself if he cannot always readily distinguish between his feelings – between those coming from his own self and those aroused by the power of the animal force.

35. For this reason, my children, never neglect your *latihan kejiwaan*, so that you may soon be able to feel and understand correctly how the forces within you are made up and how they differ. This cannot in fact be done easily – just like that – especially if it is only thought about. For, as already explained, these forces have blended with the human self to such a degree that you feel and maybe consider that they arise only from your own clean and pure inner force.

36. Because this is most likely to happen, many people who study and wish to understand this matter give up eating meat. Their purpose in doing this is just to achieve their aim quickly

– that is, to be able to separate and distinguish between what arises from their own inner self and what is effected by the animal force – and further, to come to know their eternal role and understand about the best life.

37.   Such an effort is certainly not wrong, even if it may possibly not succeed in bringing those people to the true level, for this really cannot be considered easy to attain.

38.   Many of these people, indeed, have even taken it so far that they no longer like eating meat and have got used to eating vegetables only.

39.   To those above all who make no effort whatever in this matter, and merely think about it, it will certainly become just a talking point. That is why you are reminded again and again never to neglect your *latihan kejiwaan*, in order that you may really be able to start out on the right foot or act in the right way.

40.   For on a way like this there is no longer any need for you to eat less meat or none. You continue as is normal, meaning that you go on eating in the ordinary way as people usually eat on earth. This will result in your being able to feel and be truly aware how these forces act within you, and the role of your heart will be only that of a witness. Moreover this way works in a manner that will put no strain on the parts of your body, to harm them or make you ill.

41.   Such is the fruit and outcome of the *latihan*, which truly differs from any action based merely on strength of will. So never choose a way of the latter kind, for, as has been said, behind it is only a desire of the heart, and in reality the heart is the servant of forces whose origins are still unknown to you and which might therefore thrust you in a direction you would not wish to take.

42.   That is the danger if you tackle the task wrongly. Before you are able to realize the truth, you naturally assume that all your actions, all your deeds, come from the will of your own,

human self, whereas nearly all of them still spring from the animal and other such forces. You take them as coming from your own self, of course, because within it the animal force has complete control.

43. So your state at that time poses a riddle: who is actually enthroned in your inner self for the time being? However profoundly you think about this, you will not be able to reach the level where the difference in nature between what comes from your human self and what comes from the animal force is evident.

44. This is precisely why many of us, of mankind, do not have a character attuned to the basic principle of mankind – humanity. In other words, many of us still like – have even found pleasure in – harming the lives of other people, so that their victims fall into a state of distress.

45. At times the conduct of people who behave in this way recoils on them. Even so, they do not usually take this as a reminder of their wrongdoing. On the contrary, they react like gamblers who are having a losing run – not then stopping nor wanting to stop, but going on gambling in a blaze of passion, so that they can be said to have become oblivious of both land and sea.

46. So is it when a person's entire body has been filled and fooled by the animal force. His body, by nature splendid and faultless, has in fact become simply and solely a tool of the animal and other such forces.

47. The effect of this is not confined to his own self, for his descendants will not escape it either. Such are its consequences that it truly does great harm to the man's life and to his descendants.

48. Although that is the reality, many of us human beings still have no wish to understand and be conscious of the truth about their inner self, and as a result many men and women base their marriages only on what pleases the heart.

49. Consequently, many really undesirable things happen: that is to say, many people's behaviour is out of keeping with their status as human beings, meaning that they lack the true human qualities. So these people can be said to lose completely their human *jiwa* – the perfect foundation and mainstay for that status.

50. As a result, should any of them be interested in studying, or wish to understand, the inner nature of mankind – the *kejiwaan* – their progress will be extremely slow.

8
KINANTHI

1. Such is the outcome for a man who does not care to understand or gain insight into his inner self. So when he unites with his wife he is unable to be aware of the significance of that union. In other words, his sexual relations with his wife are prompted solely by desire.

2. Of course his children cannot be preserved from the effects of of such faults. The wrong ways the parents take, their children automatically follow.

3. Such faults have been passed on from generation to generation endlessly. Hence it is better to say no more about such conduct, for it is useless to blame the parents.

4. It is enough to take such faults as an example just for yourself, so that you can prepare to begin correcting all these faults, in order to escape the pressure of forces you do not wish for.

5. In this respect, your body is like a house that has begun to be repaired and rebuilt, as well as possible, in accordance with its outer characteristics, to enable you later to be truly conscious of the real status of a human being.

6. By this means, if you meet no further obstacles, you will become healthy outwardly and inwardly.

7. When you are like that, even though you have no intention at all of correcting your parents' faults, their inner content too will be influenced spontaneously.

8. So, in other words, your progress certainly benefits your parents also, whether they wish it or not: without expecting it, they become better too.

9. Thus, the child can truly be said to be capable of raising his parents to a higher level, and they will no longer impede the growth of his real self.

10. Changing the subject now, it will be as well to show how the animal force affects people's inner feeling.

11. To make this quite clear, it is best to begin with the following question and use it to simplify the explanation.

12. Why do most village-dwellers still live frugally?

13. Usually, villagers do not often eat meat or flesh, and if they do it is mostly that of fish living in the water of the paddy fields.

14. Besides fish, they now and then eat meat of other kinds, though as a rule this is when they happen to have a celebration.

15. The fish generally eaten by villagers are those that live in the water of the paddy-fields and those that live in rivers.

16. Fish of that kind – freshwater fish – live in water and indeed are animals that exist only in water.

17. Their mode of living and their way of seeking subsistence are like those of human beings, and in reality there is no difference. They too would like to find an easy way to get all they need for their existence. In short, in their own sphere of life, with their family relationships, their condition does not differ from man's.

18. In their satisfaction at obtaining something they needed or desired, all their actions are seen to speed up and to be like the lively movements of people dancing.

19. When, however, they feel upset at failing to get something they require, they can be seen stopping again and again while they look to the right and the left, and often moving to and fro as if at a loss.

20.   The feelings of fish in the water of the paddy-fields are really no different from ours in the world of mankind. Those fish are also afflicted by conditions we would call hard and bitter, and at times too they feel joy in being alive.

21.   These fish also possess shrewdness and skill, and the feelings we have at times of lowliness and of grandeur. Similarly, too, in their society male and female can express appreciation of each other's good looks.

22.   In reality the difference between the two creatures – fish and human beings – is very great. To man, the world of fish seems limited, but to fish it is spacious.

23.   Fish find it lively and busy there. As in our human world with towns and villages and all they contain, so similar conditions exist there too, appropriate to their world.

24.   There, moreover, fish also fall ill. They are aware that death exists and that they will have to die; and many fish realize too that there is a Power governing life.

25.   Thus in their world many fish also perform their worship of God, nor do they lag behind in their way of asking or appealing for happiness in life.

26.   As to their fate when caught by men, although this is a commonplace matter to men – as it must be when fish is human food – the fish themselves feel that this is the moment fixed as their final one, the moment of their death.

27.   By comparison, this is the same as when people are taken ill and then meet their end.

28.   Such are the circumstances of fish; and although regarded by man as food to fulfil a need of his own life, fish are completely unaware of that.

29.   Now about the differences between fish that live in paddy-fields and those that live in rivers. Fish that live in rivers, besides in general being stronger and able to move

faster than those living in paddy-fields, also have feelings of broader scope.

30. Likewise in agility and courage, river fish decidedly excel the fish of the paddy-fields.

31. In other characteristics – such as stupidity, intelligence and showing off – they are almost the same.

32. That depicts the characteristics of fish in their realms. So if they influence a human being he will have traits of that sort – though the nature of his work and activities are of course different.

33. This is why many villagers work with pleasure and zeal. So industrious are they that on occasion they even take no account of time.

34. Especially when they happen to feel contented, they seem to forget their rest-breaks.

35. On the other hand, if their work is constantly criticized, they despair.

36. Sometimes even, when this happens, their minds get into such a turmoil that when next they work, or when told to go back to work, the outcome of their labour is almost useless.

37. Villagers' sense of happiness is extremely limited, so that they fear to leave the village where they were born, and go elsewhere. There are even those who are content to live in their village, although there in fact they remain short of everything.

38. To return to how fish are: though all are fish, the river kind are more deft than paddy-field fish, as a consequence of their often being swept away in floods – many even being carried a great distance owing to the swift flow of the water.

39. So, although such an event is a danger to them and a cause of suffering, they become adroit in movement.

40.	And those fish are forcibly cut off from their families by the floods, and compelled to live alone, away from the security of their families.

41.	So, if likened to us human beings, those fish have to use their minds to enable them to find a source of subsistence as quickly as possible, and they must spontaneously train their feelings, to make them firm when facing the approach of dangers and disasters such as they have experienced before.

42.	If the force of such a fish reaches a human being, that person will become resolute, his feelings will broaden, and he will stand up to whatever may befall him.

43.	He will also wish to expand his knowledge, and will not shrink from leaving the place where he was born, to go elsewhere in his own interests. Thus his situation is not like that described earlier, in which the person is simply resigned to putting up with anything, provided he may remain at his birthplace.

44.	But, good though such force may be in a fish, it is still far from what a human being needs.

45.	Because what properly should be important in human life is not merely the search for food – necessary though food certainly is – but also the wish to fulfil our essential duty to gain insight into the perfect human life.

46.	For, having gained that insight, we can soon find out for certain how the fish or animal force acts within us, and also tell one from another of the forces in us.

47.	We can also regulate those forces in an orderly way and channel them in the right directions, which can be likened to uniting the forces with their respective partners, so that they feel satisfied.

48.	Satisfying the animal force in this way opens a path for man, to enable him to go further and increase his stature as a leading creature.

49.   So, in other words, although this action by man has the nature simply of giving help, it nevertheless does not exclude the interests of his own inner self.

50.   On the other hand, however, a person will find the way dark or will dwell in darkness if he is incapable of regulating those forces in the manner described above.

51.   In darkness like that, a man's inner feeling may get into such a turmoil that the outlook proper to his human status can be said to be utterly lost.

52.   Now to change the subject: although villagers usually eat the freshwater fish spoken of earlier, they sometimes eat the flesh of chickens too.

53.   Most villagers, of course, raise chickens not for their own food but to sell in the towns. Yet at times the villagers will need some of the chickens to eat themselves.

54.   So let us give an account of the life of chickens. The way they usually seek food is by using their claws, and by habit they like looking for it in rubbish dumps.

55.   Besides seeking it in refuse, they are also given food every morning by the people who rear them. Despite this, chickens do not give up their habit of scratching for food.

56.   This is how we human beings describe the habits of chickens. But to the chickens their case is no different from the way we people work for an income by using our energy and thought.

57.   And in their realm chickens feel that they are living in spacious conditions that form a world of its own, full of all sorts of things necessary for their life, as people in our life live in busy places, such as towns, or in places free from bustle, such as villages.

58. So, too, in returning to roost every evening from their wandering, chickens are like us men coming back home every evening from where we work, to be united with all our family.

59. In their coops we see the chickens roosting in rows on perches; that too is the same as our sleeping under blankets on thick mattresses or, when those cannot be afforded, on bamboo or wooden pallets.

60. As we see it, chickens wander no further than a man's voice carries, but to the chickens this seems a very large area for their activities. An expanse wider than that seems strange to them, and they could not find their way back over it.

9
SIMOM

1. Small young chicks would get lost in such a broad expanse even more easily; therefore they flock very close to home.

2. With regard to mating, a cockerel is always seen surrounded by numerous hens, and it is also seen that hens do not mate with one cockerel only; but for chickens such a state of affairs is quite different from our view of it. In other words, for chickens in their world this situation is the same as ours is for us in the human world, where a husband marries one wife and a wife one husband.

3. Their many-coloured feathers are regarded in the chicken world in the same way as we look on other people wearing beautiful clothes or clothes of various styles.

4. Chickens only feel a family relationship while still small, so the mother hen recognizes and shows care for her offspring only while they remain small. None show any feeling of relationship with one another when the chicks have grown up, neither the chicks with their mother nor the hen with her offspring.

5. This trait in chickens – strange though we human beings think it – is quite normal in their world, because it is a requirement of their life.

6. Thus a cockerel shows no reluctance to mate with any hen, even his own mother.

7. A cockerel is not only ready to mate with his own mother, but equally to do so even with his own grandmother.

8. Strange as these habits of chickens seem to us human beings, for the chickens this is not a matter of sexual desire for mother or grandmother, but rather of mating with a true partner.

9. So much to explain the nature of chickens. When the essence of their feeling comes to affect human feelings, the person concerned will show traits like theirs, though in a different manner.

10. Now to discuss people who live in towns. In general, town people eat meat from many kinds of animals, each with its own character and habits.

11. To explain the nature and traits of so many animals one by one would certainly need a great deal of space, so it is best to explain only some of the more important points.

12. As for the others, though those characters and habits will not be recounted here, later on you will spontaneously witness in your *latihan* how those animal forces act on and affect your self; spontaneously too you will get evidence of how the influences of those forces differ from one another.

13. For town people, who have eaten a great deal of meat from an assortment of animals, it is really very difficult to detect and feel the characteristics of genuine feelings. So when their feelings stir, arousing a desire for something, these people do not and as yet cannot tell which feelings are truly their own and which come from the influence of this or that force.

14. Because their feelings are so muddled, much of what they have done has given them little benefit. It is even harder for them when they turn to the *latihan kejiwaan*, which must necessarily be accompanied by quiet, peaceful feelings.

15. That is why many who follow the *latihan kejiwaan* keep meeting frustration, meaning that they do not reach the level called that of a noble *jiwa*.

16. At times the difficulties they experience even make them feel they have lost their direction; so, in their desire to make progress, they worry whether they may be going astray. If they stop doing the *latihan*, though, they feel disappointed, because they have been doing it for a long time.

17. Such is the confusion in the feelings of town people. Even so, never forget that human nature is the nature of the perfect life, which may be likened to something that can be used to fulfil its own needs.

18. So do not worry, but keep diligent to attain a training of the self that truly gives evidence of reality.

19. Actually the animal force cannot easily exercise full sway over us human beings. Much in human nature still cannot readily be influenced by that force, provided a person takes care and does not go with the heart's avid demands.

20. To make this clear; people are affected by the animal force through heedlessness, together with their inclination at times not to behave as human beings should – in other words, to neglect to act in a truly human manner. Then just because of that neglect, their self is further urged on and affected by the animal force, with the result that at length they feel all those deeds to be right that truly are wrong, and consider their state normal.

21. Such wrongdoing means that people present the animal force with a field to work in where that force is free to do anything. The longer this goes on, the more the animal force thrives, but the people will be sure to forfeit their glory as beings created to excel.

22. Such things will happen when a person has become quite lost. Thereafter, in the animal world, this remnant of a human being will live his life like an animal, and will find it also a life of happiness and suffering.

23. In the animal realm, this former human being will no longer be able to distinguish between the animal and the human worlds, for he will no longer have the faculty for

58

this purpose, so that in the realm of animals he will already feel and understand like a creature belonging to that realm.

24. That shows what comes from the misdeeds of a person led solely by his *nafsu* of greed. So it is best for you to shun such habits and exert yourself to stop the animal force gaining mastery of your feelings and impeding your progress.

25. Failing that, not only will you be lost in the future, but affected now too, and you could also debase the *jiwa* of your descendants.

26. Now begins a brief explanation of the characters and habits of those animals whose flesh is much eaten by town dwellers; this includes fish, chickens, goats and cattle.

27. The influence of the force in fish and of that in chickens has been explained above; here will be explained only how the feelings of people who eat goat's meat and beef are affected by the forces in them.

28. Actually, town people eat many other kinds of meat, but those will not be dealt with here, for to explain about them would probably need too much space, and it is a matter, as has been said previously, that can be met with in the *latihan kejiwaan* later.

29. So let us speak about goats. In its own world, a goat's feelings and its understanding about fulfilling its life's tasks are really no different from ours in our world. The open meadow, which we see as full of vegetation, is to the goat a working area for it to obtain what is necessary for its life.

30. So what we regard as grass and foliage are to the goat an assortment of foods comparable to what we see in shops and markets.

31. In short, in their own sphere goats find quite a number of ways of organizing their joint life, so that they busy themselves working together at one task and another, just as we human beings in our world are busy buying and selling

goods necessary for life, and arranging places of entertainment, and so on.

32. Because of that similarity, people emotionally weak – and who, moreover, have never undertaken the training to enable them to be conscious of their human identity – are very easily swayed by the animal force. If this has happened already, then such people, when their end comes, will certainly be lost in the animal world.

33. That is how it is, could the truth be known; but those still blind to it have no idea of the problem of falling so far below the human level.

34. Yet so deep a fall afflicts themselves not only in their last moments; even while still living in the human body they no longer behave in a manner becoming to mankind. This is what results from their downfall; so in reality the roles are reversed, with people finding their field of life narrowed, while animals, on the contrary, attain one especially spacious.

35. In these circumstances the animal force has grown stronger and stronger and can follow up its every desire. Therefore people filled with animal force are characterized by a readiness to follow only the greed of their heart.

36. Now about the mating of male and female goats: they are like chickens, who are ready to mate with many hens, without discrimination among sister, mother, grandmother or any other.

37. Although we regard the behaviour of a goat in its world as like that of a cockerel that mates with many hens, actually this is the same thing to them as permanent human marriage is for us.

38. Thus, if people finally become lost in that world, they will also be happy. However, the happiness they find in that world is not in the least like the happiness in the human world

or realm. On the contrary, the feelings of a person filled with goat force are filled with lust.

39.   In short, his lust is like the thirst of a heavy drinker who has run out of liquor, and he feels restless and on edge unless constantly in the presence of women.

40.   The influence of the animal force has such an effect that the men taken in by it are incapable of suspecting the fact. Some even claim that sexual intercourse is only for ridding oneself of desire. In fact, though, they do not rid themselves of it, but only give in to the insistence of their desire.

10
PUCUNG

1. Some people, too, say, that such behaviour has become customary in human life, and otherwise what would be the point of living.

2. These remarks really do not call for reproach, for their impulse is the animal force that has become the content of these people's feelings. Only later, if at length their health breaks down, will they perhaps be able to feel this.

3. And only then will they see also that they have gone far wrong and feel regretfully how much better it would have been had they not behaved in such a way.

4. To go back to the habits of goats: a goat knows his shed and feels about it as a chicken about his coop. There, he is like us human beings in a house complete with furniture.

5. In lying down to sleep every night, the goat can also be compared to us lying on deep mattresses or on pallets.

6. Goats and chickens differ slightly, however, in one characteristic: a goat does not readily recognize his shed when alone.

7. For that reason goats prefer company and enjoy living in herds.

8. And if a human being comes under their influence, his disposition becomes like that too.

9. For instance, he only wants to conform, and has scarcely any standpoint or convictions of his own.

10. Moreover, goats are apt to get lost if they roam about.

11. Hence many people who raise these animals need a herdsman to tend them all the time.

12. For, without a herdsman, besides often getting lost if they stray, goats also often damage garden produce.

13. This keeps irking their owners, so in the end the goats have to be firmly tethered and fed only where they live.

14. Even the herdsman's orders are not sure to be followed by the goats. For if goats are told to go forward they usually go back, and if ordered back, go forward.

15. Such are the habits of goats.

16. Thus, if a man becomes influenced by the force of these animals, their habit of straying will make him feel like simply following his own desire in everything.

17. As for their wandering off without recognizing any limits, this makes a man's feelings unstable and his opinions always vague.

18. Thus his aims lack fixed direction, so that his views swing this way and that, which may result in him forcing himself to act along lines of whose goodness and rightness he cannot know.

19. So it is best that there should be someone to warn him, to enable him soon to be conscious of his faults, soon also to be aware of his own self.

20. Even cultivated people are not exceptions to this. For, though a person may be learned, if his feelings are still swayed by the animal force, he too gets lost. His danger is even greater, because through his very knowledge the animal force may lead him further and further astray.

21. That person is in so difficult a position that, unless he truly is conscious of it, the knowledge he has acquired will be quite useless for his life.

22. That really is so. For, as explained earlier, such knowledge exists only in the mind, and the mind is simply the servant

of his life force, into which, owing to neglect, the animal force has flowed, arousing his desire.

23.   For that reason quite a number of educated people still do not care to behave as they should, or they readily go astray.

24.   In many of them such behaviour has even become second nature, so that they no longer recognize the restraints of humanity.

25.   That is why some people say it is better to remain ignorant than to become a clever man, if his ability even adds to his suffering.

26.   But this really cannot be justified, for ignorance makes it more difficult to help people, unless by compulsion.

27.   For the fault is not in knowledge; what is really wrong is just that the feelings have come under the sway of the animal force.

28.   So it is most necessary for people to seek ability, both outward and inward.

29.   This is necessary in order that, with that ability, they can reach the highest level, so that they can understand the true use of knowledge in relation to their own human self.

30.   By this means, co-operation is created between mind and body, or inner and outer, and this can also create real stability.

31.   Otherwise the likelihood of going still further astray is strong.

32.   Changing the subject, what will now be explained is the force that comes from the flesh of cattle. The habits of cattle are far different from those of goats. Cattle are placid, they like to keep quiet, and usually they eat only grass.

33.   By nature most cattle like to do what they are told. With their strong bodies, they do not jib at any task they are called on to do.

34. Towards cows, bulls do not follow the custom of he-goats, but behave with discrimination, and evidently mate only as necessary.

35. Cow's milk is greatly needed for human health, because it embodies strong nutrients.

36. Understand, then, that if this kind of animal force influences somebody's feelings, it makes him work hard and obey orders willingly.

37. Moreover, he gladly devotes his energy to those who need it, and he has the courage, when it is needed, to face any event.

38. His sexual activity is merely normal, that is to say, moderate; hence his body will remain healthy.

39. That briefly depicts the feelings of a man affected by the animal force that comes from cattle.

40. The animal force that comes from cattle evidently has a very good effect on the human self, as is shown by such a man's behaviour not being disappointing.

11
ASMARANDANA

1.   Good though his behaviour is, however, it still falls far short if measured by the true human standard.

2.   Moreover, his goodness is still only an expression of the animal force, which of course still serves its own interest and in fact still leads human feelings astray into the animal realm.

3.   It is different if a man occupies his rightful position, which is indeed more meaningful and which can ease his progress towards perfecting his life as a human being.

4.   Then, if he is fortunate, he can rise step by step to a higher and nobler level.

5.   This explanation about the influence of the forces of matter, vegetation and animals will now be followed by one about the *jasmani* force – the force of what is generally called man's physical or coarse body.

6.   Seen in its true light, however, man's physical body cannot in fact be called *jasmani* if it is not yet filled with the *jasmani* force.

7.   Actually, what is called the *jasmani* force means wide-ranging feelings and comprehension about earthly matters.

8.   That is why a man's body is called *jasmani*. So this force is in fact a human one, or is in the man himself, and his body is then called *jasmani*.

9.   Now for the matter of how this force influences people when it is itself of human origin.

10.   Plainly, the way it exerts influence is very different from that of the animal force, for – except savages who live all their life in the jungle – people could not possibly eat their fellows. Even though they exist, savages are not yet really

people whose bodies can be called *jasmani*, and they are still spoken of as animals.

11. So then, the way the human bodily force acts is not through eating, but through the union of *jiwa* with *jiwa*, or sexual union.

12. The effect of this force on the human self is truly tremendous, but in any case this force is also a necessity of life that cannot possibly be dispensed with.

13. For the influence of the *jasmani* force makes the terms of human life all the more complete, enabling people to bring into being other creatures like themselves.

14. That is why two different natures are found, one male and the other female.

15. Thus what is called the *jasmani* force can influence a human self that is also called *jasmani*.

16. In reality the influence of this force is mightier than that of the previous forces. However, as these forces are naturally involved in every aspect of man's life and livelihood, he need have no anxiety about them, provided he can keep them in order so that they all work in co-operation.

17. The male, be it said, forms a kind of channel for the life force, which quickly arouses desire and leads him to unite with a woman.

18. The man's title to this role as channel cannot be doubted, the proof being the existence of his private part with its action and content.

19. And indeed it was by the Will of God that the male was created to become an intermediary for the substance out of which human beings will come into existence; so man is called *laki-laki*, which means one entitled to receive the current of the life force.

20.   Even so, do not misunderstand this, my children, and feel proud and powerful because of it. Never feel like that, for in reality you, the male, are only an intermediary.

21.   The male is neither more nor less than the means by which the seed of later human beings come into this world.

22.   The nature of the female, though also of the *jasmani* kind, is such that in this matter she only has to accept the seed of the future human being brought to her by the male.

23.   After that, as time goes on, the seed of this future being grows bigger and more complete in the womb, until at length it is born in human form.

24.   That is why the one who accepts the seed and carries it in her womb has been called mother.

25.   It is truly wonderful that so important an event happens in such a matter-of-fact way, and sometimes merely through desire.

26.   And also that what begins only as liquid can finally become a living thing, with a nature no different from a man's. But probably it does not surprise you, for so indeed has God decreed, that what at first has only liquid form should later become another complete human being, and also that while still in the womb this future human being should spontaneously be able to absorb from his mother the essences of her daily food.

27.   Thus the truth is that, from the moment of conception in the mother's womb until the moment of birth, the baby is affected by the influence of plant and animal forces.

28.   Because of that, a human being is familiar with food from his very beginning until the end of his life, and the woman in whose womb he is carried is known as that person's mother.

29.   It is clear, then, that the reciprocal action between the two *jasmani* or human bodily forces takes place when the male

68

and female natures are connected. This is like a contest for influence, when it becomes evident which of the two natures wins and which loses.

30. If, however, the two are of equal purity, the force innate in the male remains in him after sexual intercourse.

31. This innate force means that which comes from the force of his parents.

32. The force innate in the woman, however, spontaneously returns to the human force of her parents after intercourse.

33. And after that the man's force spontaneously fills the woman's body, so, willingly or unwillingly, she is filled with the man's force. That is why, when married, women use their husband's name.

34. In what is said above, only a good basic force is taken as an example, namely the *jasmani* or human bodily force proper to a man. In reality, however, quite a number of people, although men in outward appearance, do not yet have in them the *jasmani* or human force. Therefore, in the situation just mentioned – the connection of *jiwa* with *jiwa* – the woman's self is filled, of necessity, with a male force that is not human.

35. Such is the way the *jasmani* force works, always interacting when a man's and a woman's *jiwa* are connected. In fact, much more needs to be said about the way this force acts during the connection of *jiwa* with *jiwa*. First, however, this matter calls for further explanations about the qualities of the human body, so they will be given now.

36. Understand, then, that the nature of the human body can be likened to that of soil in its capacity and suitability – or as a basis – for growing such things as it can grow. So in order to make clear what aptness, basis or suitability the human body has for growing something that is within it, it is best to explain here briefly the qualities of soil.

37. First there is soil that quickly absorbs the water after rain and then soon grows all sorts of vegetation.

38. Soil of that sort is indeed extremely beneficial for all kinds of life, especially human life. Many people therefore cultivate it to grow things that are useful.

39. Owing to its fertility, which enables it to produce all sorts of food for human needs, this soil is called golden earth.

40. In terms of the human body, this soil is like the best of bodies, that have the capacity or the basis to receive extensive knowledge of the *kejiwaan* and also to demand outer knowledge of wide scope.

41. If a person with a body of this quality receives knowledge of the *kejiwaan*, he will soon be able to show the fruit or result of his receiving and then give guidance to others who are in need of it.

42. So, also, if he absorbs or studies some wordly subject, when fully versed in it he will soon be able to apply his ability to the needs of society.

43. Society pins its hopes on just such people, for, besides having special abilities from which the community benefits, they also have inner stability.

44. So greatly therefore do they benefit society that they can be said to give life to people who, through having experienced the dark side of life, are almost dead.

45. The fertility of that soil may be said to be due to the fact that the powers of fire, air, water and earth influence it equally.

46. This is the circumstance that produces soil that is fertile and truly to be considered excellent.

47. Such soil also owes its nature to its being surrounded by mountains, which can provide the elemental forces in balanced strength.

48. In a human self resembling this soil the powers of the *nafsu* of anger, greed, patience and acceptance are well balanced.

49. In addition, this soil is surrounded by many mountains, and for the human self they represent the highest powers, which always envelop such a man's inner feeling.

50. That is why people of this kind will do nothing to betray the highest standards.

12
PANGKUR

1. Thus they differ greatly from those people who only do what the heart wishes and trust only in the saying 'Where there's a will there's a way'.

2. Now to discuss the properties of clay. As well as not letting water sink into it quickly after rain, this kind of soil is apt to cling to whatever touches it.

3. Even so, soil of this quality is counted among the best, for it too can sustain all kinds of growth and become a bed for growing many sorts of useful plants, thus being of benefit to human life.

4. People with qualities like this kind of soil scarcely differ from the first group. If they receive knowledge of the *kejiwaan*, it will not be long before they too are able to show some fruit or result of their receiving. And at length they too are able to give guidance to other people who need it.

5. Besides that, they are also capable of receiving the flowering of the talents of their *jiwa*; for instance, in all forms of culture, which in time they can use in the service of society.

6. Their one shortcoming is that when helping other people they still exert some hold on them. And also when something goes wrong they are apt to drag other people into it.

7. As to the nature of clay, the elemental forces of fire, air, water and earth carried in it are not evenly balanced. Of these four, the forces of fire and air are stronger than those of water and earth. But another good point about this soil is that it is largely found near rivers.

8. Continuing the comparison with people whose qualities are like those of clay, the forces of the *nafsu* of anger and greed are stronger in them than those of the *nafsu* of patience and acceptance. So everything they do is still encompassed by the *nafsu* of anger and greed.

9.   Despite that, however, these people, because they have feelings that are alive – that is, comparable to the quality of soil found near rivers – are not seriously misled by the power of the *nafsu* of anger and greed.

10.   There is another kind of soil besides these – muddy soil. Its feature is that rain sinks very slowly into it and so in the course of time this soil gives off a foul vapour.

11.   Soil of this sort, however, can also grow things, ranging from trees of great girth to very slender ones. The fruit of the small one is mainly of little use to mankind. For the most part only the large trees bear fruit that makes a useful addition to man's standard of living.

12.   This can be picked only once a year or, properly speaking, only once a year do these trees bear fruit. Such is the capacity of muddy soil. Comparing people with this soil, when they receive any inner knowledge, the knowledge received comes to rest for a very long time in the sphere of thought.

13.   This is why many people are good only at thinking and talking, and others claim ability which they show no evidence of or do not yet possess. Nevertheless, later on they also may produce something real, and this could be some small help to those who need to deepen their knowledge of the *kejiwaan*.

14.   So the outcome may also be not unsatisfactory, provided the insight they have received is not kept too long in the mind. For if that happens, what they know will well and truly confuse other people, because it will be just chatter.

15.   Continuing about the nature of this soil, it contains the elemental forces coming from fire and air in greater strength

than those from water and earth, especially as it is located far from rivers and mountains.

16. This indicates that, in people comparable to this soil, the power of the *nafsu* of anger and greed is stronger than that of the *nafsu* of patience and acceptance. So when such people want to fulfil some need they act too hastily.

17. All the more so if they never get really good advice or guidance from other people; then such behaviour will be carried to excess.

18. So may be explained the condition and capacity of people whose characteristics are like those of muddy soil.

19. Now to turn the discussion to another kind of soil – *padas*, a hard, unbroken soil. When it is raining what falls on this soil immediately runs in every direction, and if there are hollows it is trapped in them as in bowls, and hence in time this water too gives off a stench.

20. Furthermore, what grows in such soil is mostly a type of grass; but other things grow there too, mainly large trees, some with thorny trunks.

21. In this soil the forces that come from fire and air are far greater than those from water and earth.

22. Also, as such soil is usually located far from rivers, it gets water only from rainfall.

23. Thus, if people comparable to this type of soil receive insight, they do not then set it to work or quickly put it into practice, but scatter it in all directions instead. That is to say, they like talking about their receiving to other people, and also greatly enjoy being praised as vigilant and wise.

24. Owing to the pleasure this gives them, they talk in a high-flown way to almost everybody about what they know, though as yet unable to realize what kind of knowledge they have received.

25. Even so, this is better than keeping to themselves the knowledge or guidance they have received. For perhaps some of their listeners may be able to realize what is being spoken of.

26. In truth, people of this nature have a very small capacity for receiving any insight that would be of much real use for their life.

27. Even though at times they seem to develop, it is not in a way suited to their original content; on the contrary, this development may lead them into wrongdoing.

28. The more so, indeed, because they are already filled with the mightly forces of the *nafsu* of anger and greed; so their conduct goes from bad to worse.

29. Now there is one more kind of soil to be explained: sandy and dusty soil. When it rains, the water quickly sinks through this soil, which in consequence grows hardly anything.

30. If anything grows there, it is mostly some kind of grass, and even this cannot long survive at times of drought.

13

DHANDHANGGULA

1.   People comparable to soil of this kind will just not be able to produce anything of great worth. Even so, some of them rise to the point of finding the path to the right way of life.

2.   Only, even if they receive indications of what is right and useful for them it is usually almost impossible for them to develop anything of high quality.

3.   This case scarcely differs from that of stony or rocky ground, already used for comparison. Clearly, what grows from such a self is nothing but a cleverness that conflicts with nobility.

4.   Moreover, the *nafsu* whose power nearly fills their self are those of anger and greed. This being so, they behave with almost no patience or acceptance, and do not scruple to follow courses harmful to others.

5.   Thus may the characteristics of people and of soils be compared. Similarly, then, a man's efforts to improve his content will resemble the cultivation and irrigation of soil.

6.   Now, having explained the similarities between the qualities of man's body and those of soil, let us go on again with the explanation of how the *jasmani* or human force influences people in whom this force is present.

7.   So that it may be realized how one human being influences another, it has already been said that mankind is of two sexes, though their circumstances are the same – meaning that both have parts of the body that can be used for the needs of mankind. The two sexes are the male nature and the female nature.

8. When these two unite sexually, there is always an interaction of forces between them; and so, if at that time they really feel or receive it, a truth will become evident – which of the two yields to or is brought under the sway of the other.

9. Truly, it will become apparent there and then what the inner self of each is like, so far as in the act of union the *jiwa* is able to be free from other forces; that is, from forces lower than human. Certainly, no method is necessary to achieve this, for a method of any sort can only arouse the power of the *nafsu*. Instead, what is needed in these circumstances is to abandon all the forces of the *nafsu* and just to experience that the feeling is alive, with thought given up, as during the *latihan*.

10. Of course, if seen outwardly, with the ordinary eyes, the sexual union of two people appears as one human being with another human being; but in fact each may still be filled with forces that easily degrade the level of the human *jiwa*. The inner content of people in olden times was more stable, so it was normal for them to say that a human body contained a human *jiwa*, for of course they had not then experienced conditions like those of today.

11. Moreover, people then had fewer contacts with others than people have today. Nowadays there is much more work to do and we have to make no little use of the mind. That is why the existence of people of former times cannot possibly be equated with that of people now.

12. So, too, the inner content of many people nowadays is unlike that of people of old, who were simply human, outwardly and inwardly, and ruled solely by human force; so each of us has still to discover what our inner content is.

13. Could we be truly conscious, however, we would not find such a state of affairs hard to believe, for in the present age we come up against much more that can sap the force of our inner self.

14. To make this clear, it would be best to depict here how it is for them when a young bachelor and a virgin girl marry who are alike filled with the human force. This illustration can really be taken as the ideal. For a man who happens to be able to find such a marriage can quickly make apparent between the two a living bond, solid and strong, which fills and unites them with one and the same force – the human force.

15. A man always seeks just that kind of marriage, because at the time of sexual union the force in the two bodies can readily merge, so that inwardly the two natures no longer have any sense of separateness. For that reason a woman is often referred to as *garwa*, meaning half of her husband's soul or life and that is also why a married woman goes under her husband's name.

16. Besides peace and harmony, a further result of that marriage is that it opens the way towards a life of prosperity. If they beget a child of that marriage, the force of the human seed coming through the man's self will awaken his bodily feelings.

17. And when those feelings are thus aroused he will immediately feel where the desire comes from, and he will also be able to be aware of his condition during the union, so that this will be an inner opening for him.

18. Thereafter he will be led little by little to recognize all the characteristics of his ancillary forces or of the forces that are continually uniting and separating within his self.

19. Therein too he will always get indications enabling him gradually to become more familiar with his ancillary forces and other forces; and it may then be said that he is more capable of remaining detached from them, still uniting and being united with them but not bound or swayed by them.

20. This is how it should be, but in fact it very rarely is so, for people – especially the young – usually do not want, as yet, to be aware of the forces within them. The choice of a girl

to marry as a life partner is not made from the viewpoint of the *kejiwaan*, but is based on everyday social contacts whose content only brings their hearts closer together.

21. For that reason, a good way to become conscious of the qualities of the forces within you and also of those in a woman is to find a means, if you can, whereby you immediately experience the distinction between the heart and mind and the inner feeling.

22. By this means your inner feeling will recognize for the first time the genuine forces whose source is your self, and next you will recognize also the action of other forces that previously deceived your inner feeling, making you merely their tool.

23. Many people, being the tools of these forces, do not behave as they should. These forces were indeed embodied in a person's inner feeling from his beginning, when still in his mother's womb, until the day of his birth, and continue until the last moment of his life. Thus it is truly not fitting and proper when anybody behaves with these forces unregulated. A person must first put these forces into a state that no longer impedes him; only then will he behave in accordance with his own right. He should not trust his conduct solely to his own courage.

24. For acting in this random way is highly likely to cause errors, leading to the loss of his human force and – unless he is lucky – much further suffering. So, to avoid these big mistakes, never neglect the simple, good way described above; or if you have not yet encountered it, make the effort to enable you to find it.

25. Now to take another example: suppose a young man filled with human force marries a girl containing forces lower than the human, but that both are conscious of their own situation, or the husband at least is aware of his, then, when these two unite, the man's force will finally dominate them

both and the lower forces in the woman will spontaneously disappear and be replaced by her husband's human force.

26. So the result will be no different from that described earlier. But even though the force within him is human, if the husband is not yet really master of it he will not be able to maintain his status.

27. There is another reason too, connected with his ignorance, as yet, of the content of his inner self. The forces which have become associated with his life still greatly hamper his progress towards perfection. And for that reason too his original content may suffer such a collapse as to be of no more use to him.

28. If likened to a man who owns tools for working, then he is one who cannot yet understand their use; so they are no help to him, but a heavy burden rather, and maybe this burden will become heavier and bring disaster on him if some of the tools have dangerous features.

29. Likewise in matters of the *kejiwaan*. Although in reality the forces within a person's self have the nature of ancillaries or aides, if he handles them wrongly through lack of understanding, these aides act in the opposite way and become hindrances or obstacles to his well-being. For that reason many people suffer errors and events they would not wish for.

30. Similar is the case of a husband as yet unconscious of the *kejiwaan* whose wife is pregnant. At times he behaves wrongly, being apt to have sexual relations with other women. The reason for this is that usually a pregnant woman strongly dislikes complying with her husband's frequent desire for intercourse. So her husband, perhaps unable to control his passion, feels compelled to have intercourse with another woman.

31. In the end he will feel disappointed, for sexual intercourse with the other woman will pull down the level of his own

content. Yet, if only he knew the truth, his wife's refusal is not solely by her own wish, but also by the wish of the child in her womb, who in reality is warning his parents to be patient and to surrender, in order that all the while he is in the womb he will be well and happy.

32.   Such is the meaning of the wife's refusal, rightly understood. Clearly, then a warning of this kind must be heeded, so that the condition of the child still in the womb remains good and happy. Then his wife's and his own self will also remain in a state of well-being and happiness. But usually people do not pay attention to this as yet, or do not yet understand it. So they still behave wrongly, as has been described, without being in the least concerned. Some of them even go so far as to consider this just a normal custom, and thus gladly have sexual relations with women who have long been the target of such erotic passion.

33.   That is how the forces in a man's self work, with the result that he does not feel his behaviour is wrong, but even considers it right.

34.   Some men too feel even that such conduct is a mark of superiority, for it is a reminder of their masculinity. Yet in fact it greatly impairs their status as human beings, creatures of high level.

35.   Furthermore, if that is not soon realized, the wrongdoing may go on and on, making it in the end very hard for a man to return to the high level proper to him.

36.   The more so if, after that, he still wants sexual intercourse with his pregnant wife. This intercourse may make his child and wife suffer, as well as himself, with the result that they, who have had no part in all this, also will be affected and burdened by the mistakes he has made.

37.   His child and wife will suffer even more if such behaviour leads to him getting a disease from women who have become

targets of erotic passion. For the nature of the disease he carries will ravage his child and wife both physically and spiritually.

38. That is what will happen. Yet, as may be recalled, his wife certainly never wanted a thing like that to happen. Plainly, then, such conduct is in truth simply maltreatment of the wife and her child; so the hope of getting a child of excellent character cannot possibly be fulfilled.

39. Do realize, my children, that the *jasmani* force has so powerful an influence on people because, of course, human force is confronted with human force. And what is more, much that happens is not just human force confronting human force, but human force confronting other forces veiled by a human mask. Especially if what veils a woman's nature is a beautiful face, then a man may readily entrust himself to her and so be led anywhere by her. In truth, however, this is not only the woman's fault, but the man's too. Indeed, if seen as it actually is, the fault is mainly rooted in the man.

40. For this reason it is best as a human being not to neglect the training of the feeling, much spoken of earlier. For through this training of the feeling he becomes adept in how to receive and how to regulate the forces within him. Hence in doing anything, and especially in uniting with his wife, he will find no difficulty in separating the feeling of his inner self from other forces that always gather with it, and he will also be able to direct those forces into the channels where they belong. As this is done, the various needs of these forces are separated; for example, the need of the human force for the human force, and the needs of the other forces for those forces. So, automatically, the human force will face only the human force, and the other forces will face forces of their own kind.

41. To come to know what is explained above, it seems there is no other way than that a man must be able to lay aside his heart and mind and imagination, which usually likes groping about in what is unreal.

42. For when he is not filled with thoughts and fancies, or in other words, when he has been able to empty himself of all the thinking and imagining that usually occupy his feelings every day, he will soon receive a state from within that is felt as a vibration throughout the body and feels like the touch of a power never experienced before. This receiving will certainly progress in the course of time, until eventually he can recognize the content of his inner feeling and also know the character, use and activity of that content.

43. And in spite of the heart and mind being inactive and powerless at the time of receiving, their real role will also be seen. In that state a man is able to feel that the heart and mind are really just a servant of the forces in his inner feeling, and he also perceives, with deep regret, all the faults in his past deeds and conduct.

44. That is why the heart and mind are not to be relied on and cannot stand on their own. As explained, their role is simply and solely that of servant, and their appointed place should only be in the train of the inner self.

45. If a comparison is made with a lamp, the burning flame is its characteristic, while the oil is the force that fills the inner feeling and empowers the heart and mind to work. Clearly, then, the brightness or dimness of the lamplight depends just on the oil. Likewise, whether the heart and mind work well or badly, right or wrongly, depends just on the quality of the force that becomes the content of the inner feeling.

46. That is why, as has been said here often, the heart and mind cannot be used to become aware of one's human identity. The reason for this, as has been stated, is that their nature is simply to serve whatever commands them; or in other words, they only act and work when there is something that moves or activates them. It is fortunate if what stirs and works them is the highest power; otherwise they are sure to lose the best human way of life. That is why many people make mistakes which they claim to be correct, or act wrongly in the belief that they are doing right.

47. Thus it seems it will not be easy for a man to tell right from wrong in his behaviour except when he gets free from his heart and mind which have been fuelling his inner feeling. This done, the true state of affairs is clear – what it may be that keeps driving his inner feeling toward his heart and mind.

48. Because of this difficulty it often happens that many people do not realize what they are doing, while others act after careful thought, yet, as is plain in the end, they too go astray. This state of affairs derives in fact from the nature of the heart and mind. So it is really essential for you to be diligent in following the *latihan kejiwaan* in the manner spoken of earlier.

49. For eventually, by sincerely following the *latihan kejiwaan,* you will not employ your mind wrongly, and so the mind, which you have developed in the usual way, really will be used for your self.

50. Unquestionably it is very useful for a man to apply himself to mental study, and the more wide-ranging the better, provided his study serves as a tool only for his human self, not for a self filled with lower forces – a condition that can cause people very great suffering.

51. Now to change the subject. Before binding themselves in marriage, many young men often like to have sexual relations with women, some even making a habit of it, as though it was considered a recreation because it could relieve sexual passion. To others, to act in this way even seems a necessity, in order to satisfy their sexual desire before they have a permanent, lawful wife.

52. This is the same sort of mistake as made by men already married who still like to behave in that way. In other words, such conduct is nothing but that of a man who simply spoils and soils his own inner feeling. Of course men who cannot yet realize this regard it as normal, and thus feel it is merely a form of pleasure. But the truth is that such behaviour is extremely dangerous, especially for young men, who by nature, broadly speaking, will when they are married become channels for the seed of those who will come into being later. For pleasure of this kind is not easy to give up – it cannot be done just like that! – and moreover it is not an ordinary pleasure, but, incited as it is by low forces, gives rise to boundless inner suffering.

53.   As stated earlier, the sexual union of men and women is in reality a struggle of forces that determines which of them will win, which will be defeated. So to feel and believe that such an activity is something ordinary and just a pleasure cannot be justified in the least.

54.   So it is best to keep well clear of conduct and habits of that kind, for it is certainly true that they damage one to the *jiwa*.

55.   That is why people who have sexual intercourse are said to be of one *jiwa*. It is quite clear, then, that conduct of that kind is not an amusement, but behaviour that results only in harming the *jiwa*.

56.   A man will therefore feel deep remorse when he is able to perceive for himself all that has happened. For the damage suffered almost throughout his inner feeling can then really be seen.

57.   He will also feel deep remorse when he discovers how his handsome and manly outer qualities, which he has used to lend himself distinction and superiority, have become filled with a low force unfit to be the content of a human inner feeling. Thus the qualities contained in his inner feeling make a picture quite alien to his own view.

58.   So far-reaching are the results of that fault. Clearly, then, his habit of having sexual relations with women whose inner feeling is already ruined spoils almost all his qualities,

changing his character to one far different from its original nature.

59.   Even in such a case, however, sometimes a man will not forget the importance of his life – that is, he will still feel the need for a young woman to become his life partner, and will also wish to get a child from that marriage, who may be counted on in time to succeed him or to be a link with his existence. Indeed, men with just that sort of experience are cleverer at choosing good-looking and well-formed girls from nice families.

60.   That really is the right way – the way in which a man would choose a bride. For by marrying a woman like that, first, his heart and feelings will be satisfied because of his wife's outward beauty; second, his heart and feelings will also become peaceful, because before him and beside him he will have a wife of good character; lastly, he will have high hopes of begetting a child with the best qualities.

14

KINANTHI

1. For a young man who has behaved wrongly before marriage, however, the possibility of experiencing so good a state of affairs can scarcely be said to exist. His errors have been such that sexual relations with him cause havoc to the content of his wife's inner feeling, which also finally meets a fate like her husband's.

2. Thus does it happen that their hopes for their life to go well in the future are dimmed. This is a man's reward who acts only from desire, debasing what should be a good state.

3. Inevitably the low, depraved forces flowing from the husband have a terrible effect on his wife, soiling and degrading the once clean and pure content of her inner feeling.

4. The husband just does not think of his behaviour as corrupting, for his heart has become an instrument of the low, debased forces which entered into him before marriage, when he took pleasure in associating sexually with women filled with such forces.

5. So although in reality his conduct is destructive, nevertheless he feels it only as right and worthy.

6. Such is the fate of a man whose inner feeling – because of his own misdeeds – has been duped by low forces.

7. For this reason, if a man's inner feeling has been too long ensnared by low forces, his awareness has also been affected, and so what to him seems awareness really remains enveloped by the dark clouds of those forces.

8. This being so, neither his good looks nor even his mind are free from the grip of those forces.

9.   So later on, when he begets a child, his child will also be swayed by those low forces and will have a character very different from that which his father had when still young and pure.

10.   This is why a child or person can be filled with forces differing from or not matching those of his ancestors.

11.   Because of this, the child will eventually have to suffer a great deal during his life, especially in becoming aware of his human identity.

12.   The reason is just that almost the whole content of the child's inner feeling has been affected by the low forces, thus causing his thoughts always to be directed to the interests of those forces.

13.   That is also the reason why there is scarcely any likelihood that thinking can be used to become aware of the true content of the inner feeling.

14.   As a result, many of those interested in this subject fail in the end to reach their goal for the very reason that they still use thought as the essential means for doing so.

15.   Therefore, without suspecting it, not a few of them veer in another direction and so claim as truth what is really error. The situation is thus turned upside down, and actions certainly wrong for the human force are yet claimed to be right, by the will of the forces which are fooling the mind.

16.   Clearly, in circumstances like that, it is the person concerned who is at fault. The fact is that in man's original state those forces will not and indeed need not encroach on the position of the human force, for their nature is actually just that of ancillaries. But since the man himself cannot restrain his *nafsu*, those forces make their own way into his inner feeling for the pleasure of occupying a place where they feel happier than in their own place.

17. But the man, having too long behaved wrongly, is finally made powerless and forced to give up all that belongs to him – from his inner feeling to his thinking – leaving those forces to make free use of it.

18. Of course, the way those forces use his properties accords not with human standards but with their own standards; so the man's inner feeling and his thinking are forced down into a state of degradation.

19. This illustrates what happens when those forces have gained mastery in a person's inner feeling. A man not yet aware of his inner feeling supposes that, however he behaves, it is bound to stay clean and unchanged. So, feeling only pleasure and enjoyment, he associates with attractive women who have often and for a long time mixed with all sorts of other men. Such are the circumstances of a man's life, including what goes on within him. So be assured that thought cannot possibly be used to find the truth about this.

20. In sum, then, to be able to know the truth of this to the point of having real understanding, there seems to be no alternative so easy as a way whereby the self is trained without having to arouse thought and imagination.

21. The training, however, need not be described here, because much has been said about it earlier.

22. For a woman too this is important, because after following the training in earnest she will be able to know the content of her inner feeling with all its ancillary forces.

23. Thus, eventually, in sexual relations with her husband the content of her inner feeling will not become the target of the low forces picked up by him through his association with other women.

24. Moreover, provided her *latihan* enables her to reach the level needed for a woman's role, she will be better developed and hence able to separate those forces correctly and channel them into their proper directions.

25. That point can be illustrated by the example of oil that is put with water. Although a person has the forces of matter, vegetation and animals all gathered together in him, each will separate spontaneously from the others and quickly flow towards its rightful destination.

26. Nevertheless, in receiving the feeling of passionate love, neither person will be disappointed; only, those who may be called channels of that passion cannot attain to the level known as 'of one *jiwa*' – meaning that the husband's *jiwa* is united with his wife's. It may very likely be that in this they will fall short of the ideal, which is that sexual union between husband and wife is in reality a *jiwa* union and so accords with that term 'of one *jiwa*'.

27. However, this case is far different from that described earlier, because the aspect of rejection that has its place in this sexual union is something that arises of itself from the inner feeling, and in reality defends the self against the low forces brought by her husband.

28. For that reason, such a reaction by the wife is indeed not wrong; on the contrary, it is truly proper and praiseworthy.

29. In fact, that action safeguards not only her own inner self, but even that of her husband as well, because it enables him also to escape from the sway of the low forces.

30. A husband who has a life partner like that is truly most fortunate, because his wife is not only a partner skilled at managing household affairs, but she can also purify, or at least help to purify, her husband's inner state, which has been affected by low forces.

31. A woman ought to be like this, so that her attractive appearance and good family background are not wasted. Rather, in such circumstances her repute will grow in fragrance

and she will become increasingly fitted for other women to take as an example.

32. Truly, a woman fortunate enough to have a being like that is blessed. It is therefore her duty to look after her outward appearance as well and carefully as possible, so that the outer may be absorbed into the inner. With such qualities she seems, as is commonly said, like a goddess come down from heaven.

33. So she will regret it later if, for some reason, she is unable to fulfil those good qualities.

34. For if she cannot match her behaviour to her pleasing outer features, then the attractiveness and good breeding that are hers will not be able to make her life happy.

35. This is especially so if the matter has gone too far for there to be any chance of remedying it, for she will then bring on herself even greater misfortune, because her charms will increasingly be exploited by the low forces which have filled and swayed her inner feeling and her heart and mind.

36. As a result, her attractiveness, outwardly radiant, becomes in the end only a veil over the low forces hidden within her. Here lies the danger for the man who acts without earnestly assessing the matter in his feelings, or for the man who is not yet conscious of the way of the *kejiwaan*. Not a few women who are attractive and perhaps also from good families have gone astray by doing only what pleases their heart, selling themselves to men who want them.

37. In the presence of such an influence, a man who cannot control his sexual passion feels that an opportunity is offered, and so, without giving a thought to his family, he just yields to the pressure of the low forces that are disguised by a pretty face and a shapely body.

38. Generally a man's feelings weaken when he faces such a situation. Therefore his inner feeling and his mind can easily be swayed by the low forces so that of course his emotions and thought become powerless to consider further what the consequences will be.

39. The result is that only after undergoing both outward and inward suffering will he remember that error. But the woman, as soon as she can see that her prey has come to such a state, unhesitatingly abandons him, then contentedly goes on to look for another target as yet unspoilt.

40. Usually the person easily misled by the influence of low forces veiled by attractive looks is a man still young and lacking in relation to matters of the *kejiwaan*. Especially if the charmer can entice him with honeyed words, then all his feelings will be more readily taken in, impelling him to give himself up to her outwardly and inwardly.

41. Yet this case does not differ from the one just mentioned, in that the charmer will not scruple to abandon this young man also when he has experienced a fate like that of the man referred to above.

42. Such is the outcome of a man's conduct when he follows only his passion or when he is as yet unaware of the way of the *kejiwaan*; so, without him suspecting it, his fine body becomes in truth simply and solely an organ of the low forces.

43. In such circumstances the low forces feel extremely fortunate, for they can array themselves in and make use of the qualities of a human body, which are much superior to their own. But for such a man, on the contrary, it means that he is self-destructive and hence is forced to suffer, both outwardly and inwardly, the debasing of his life.

44. The nature of the outer harm he suffers can be discovered with the aid of physicians; but the inner damage can be perceived only with the help of his own self, if he is able to have his inner feeling trained.

45. That is why it is found that many of those who undertake the training feel during the *latihan* as though they are suffering from a bodily ailment and also that they are not making much progress in the *latihan*.

46. But it is best for those following the training not to feel this deeply, for it is all in the past, and so it is no use regretting it any longer except by improving their present and future conduct.

47. Clearly, then, their earlier behaviour was really and truly wrong, thus forcing the self, which ought to be unimpaired, to suffer damage, beginning with the content of the inner feeling and spreading to the outer limits – that is, to the body.

48. Such is the way the low forces in human guise influence a man, or how a person filled with low forces influences one filled with human force, and the other way round. So it seldom happens as yet that a person filled with human force meets, as he should, another person also filled with human force. Yet, as has been said a little earlier, this is really what is necessary, for in this balanced condition a man can soon unify his content and will thereby be able to assume his human identity.

49. Achieving this will be extremely difficult for a man who has sexual relations with a woman only because of his appetites and without understanding beforehand what actually happens during erotic passion.

50. However, the feelings of a man already conscious of these things are not likely to suffer from any difficulty in this matter, for by himself he will reach a level where he cannot be influenced by a person filled with the *jasmani* force or with the other, the low forces.

15
MIJIL

1. So, to make it clear, the obstacle to the perfect union of the content of the inner feeling of man and woman is, as stated above, not the nature of the man's body but the low forces which that body comes to contain.

2. Likewise, what can isolate the influence of all those low forces is not the body nor the man, but the great power that is felt to be in contact with the inner feeling after the mind stops working.

3. Be certain, then, that the man will not be able to rid himself of those low forces, for they are indeed his ancillary forces and have gathered in his being.

4. This will be the same for the woman too.

5. Hence it would seem that it is no longer useful if a man, because he needs a better life, forces himself to go away to some lonely place far from other people.

6. Similarly, it would seem to be of no use if men intentionally keep away from women and women from men. For in truth both are in the same situation, so a man's intention to have nothing more to do with women means just the same as if he could have nothing more to do with his own self; it is the same also for a woman.

7. So in reality there is no need for the two to wish to keep apart from each other.

8. Moreover God has willed that the union of men and women is required during their earthly life so that they may pass on the human seed.

9. This is in order that their descendants may spread over the earth and then everywhere adorn it with the variety of things they devise.

10. And that they may also make use of the world as a place to nurture the self both outwardly and inwardly.

11. For that reason they need to deepen and widen their knowledge, so that with knowledge of such scope they may get what they need for a happy life.

12. Furthermore, deep and wide-ranging knowledge makes it easier to organize society, so that it can be made peaceful and prosperous.

13. By this means too is created collective harmony wherein many people would help one another.

14. For instance, the talented ones would be willing to teach those still backward; the wealthy would not hesitate to give aid to the needy; and the strong would be glad to help those still weak. With conditions like that, the world we live in would truly be a noble and excellent place.

15. Besides that, the people would not neglect the way to guide their inner feeling towards their own self, thus making their standpoint firmer and so enabling them to have lives of outward and inward happiness.

16. As for the way to raise one's self up, it is a way that has become a commonplace for anyone who wants to carry it out. It is done by turning off the *nafsu* and thought until a state arises so truly quiet and peaceful that it cannot be described.

17. Such indeed is the way a person guides his inner feeling in that direction; it is far different from how he pursues scientific knowledge, which requires the utmost use of the mind.

18. Therefore those who follow this *latihan kejiwaan* will not use their thought in it; rather, they will need to empty out everything they imagine and think, so that they can then receive the Grace of God which already envelops them.

19. Thus it is; so what is found in that training of the inner-feeling has no trace of anything conceived by heart, imagination or mind.

20. The result of doing this is that they get evidence by which they can clearly and plainly be aware of all the forces that have become obstacles to their inner development.

21. Through the evidence obtained, difficulties that had always been met in the training of the inner feeling disappear, for the low forces that had obstructed their inner feeling separate themselves off and then take up their original places with contentment and joy.

22. So is it if a man can follow the *latihan* properly. Moreover, precisely because of this, the life force present in his inner feeling transforms him, enabling him to take his place again as an exalted and noble creature.

23. And after that he will remain firmly the controller and regulator of all his ancillary forces.

24. Especially in the man's sexual union with his wife will he no longer be affected by the low forces; hence the content of his inner feeling can then unite with that of his wife and raise it to a higher level – the level, that is, of a complete human being.

25. Thus it is clearly not the bodily nature that has to be separated from his own self but the content of that nature. So too, that which can take him to a high level is not something that exists in any particular place but something that truly always envelops his self wherever he may be.

26. This is an illustration of the true aim of the training done by a person who compels himself to do it and extinguishes all his *nafsu* and thinking – something really difficult and heavy for people in the present age.

27. Of course in earlier ages people could train their inner feeling in that way, for in distant times man's life was still simple and the conditions around him were evidently extremely quiet.

28.   Moreover, the ways of finding a livelihood were far fewer than they are today, so the possibility of carrying out such training was far greater.

29.   This is why people nowadays cannot readily undertake that kind of training of the inner feeling. So to meet this need it is better to seek a path or way which does not require giving up everyday necessities.

30.   And a way too that does not require them to isolate themselves and sit meditating in solitary places such as sea shore or river bank, mountain or forest.

16
SINOM

1. Thus people no longer need to repeat the ways of training the inner feeling used in earlier times. For they have now made so much progress in the way they arrange to meet their life needs that many places which used to have the appearance of dense jungle have now become villages and towns; many former valleys have become neat and orderly roadways; many coastal places, where once men saw only the swell of the ocean waves and heard only the sound of their booming as they struck the rocks, have now become shipping harbours or bathing resorts.

2. But what is meant by places where a man can purify his inner feeling are not the natural places referred to above. In other words, what is meant by a mountain is not the mountain of earth that can be seen anywhere, but the mountain of feeling in the breast – that is, in what is called the inner heart.

3. What is meant by forest and plain is likewise not to be taken literally, but as the place of thinking, which is in the head – that is, the brain. What is meant by ocean and river is really the feeling throughout the human body, and what is called a river is really also the flow of feeling in the sex organs. As to the meaning of why a man needs to practise asceticism in the places referred to – first on a mountain, which is actually a mountain of feeling or the inner heart – it is simply to enable him to check the force of his imagination, which usually likes to delude itself with the unreal. And the forest, which in fact is the place of thought, or the brain, is where asceticism is needed to enable him to restrain also the force of his mind, which is usually worrying about one thing or another. Again, ocean shore and river bank, which are truly the feeling throughout the body and the flow of feeling in the sex organs, are where asceticism is needed to enable him to withstand the force of his erratic feelings and to check too the power of the erotic passion with its habitual strong liking for sexual intercourse.

4. That is the true meaning of those things. Clearly, then, such things are just parables pregnant with well-hidden meanings. But parables have an advantage, for usually, if such things are said in a realistic way, the listener does not even pay attention, considering them commonplace. It is another matter when expressed as above: meaning that if a person wishes to clean the inner feeling as well as possible he needs to quieten the self on a mountain, on the seashore, or in a forest. Then he will take this more to heart and follow it up more earnestly, even though the eventual results are no different from those attainable in his own home. But there are also stories intentionally written by their authors to enable the reader to understand or to want to understand that a man can achieve happiness in his life only if he always acts honestly and in harmony with his own self. On the other hand, a man will be forced to undergo degradation and hardship in his life if he acts only according to his *nafsu* of anger and greed or if he does anything dishonestly and not in harmony with his own self.

5. Therefore it is best for the reader of storybooks, both those composed in chanting rhythm and those written in prose, to feel truly the meaning of their content. If it still is difficult for him to feel and understand, let him ask some friend who can interpret them, so that in the end he will not stay permanently skilled just at reading and chanting, but will truly be able to realize the meaning contained in the stories dressed up in those puzzling words.

6. There are even many stories too where the characters and the villages they come from, with all the circumstances and events described in them, are drawn solely from imagination and thought, not from real life. But, through the skill of the authors, many readers suppose that the contents of those stories are true, and the people told of are also thought real.

7. For this reason, among the readers are to be found those who copy the behaviour of a character described in a story and do not hesitate to put into practice his means of finding truth, by withdrawing to live quietly in a forest, on a mountain, or beside sea or river. They may even believe from what is printed in the storybook that those places really are places of worship for finding truth, and hence that at length they may possibly meet some god from the Hindu heaven who can guide them towards the right path for their life.

8. They even think that those actions will truly lead to the realization of what they have read, where much is told of knights meeting nymphs from paradise.

9. Such are the mistakes of people who cannot yet understand the true meaning of what is said in the storybooks they read. It is a very different matter with people who have been able to realize the truth, so that such things are seen to be only symbolic and that, to get evidence of the real nature of the inner self, it suffices to stay at home leading an ordinary life, provided that all the *nafsu*, the imagination and thought can be purified in the right way.

10. By doing this they are even able to look closely into whether the content of these stories is true or not, and also to see whether the author when writing them could set aside the influence of the low forces within his self.

11. In fact the author himself can of course be quite blinded by the constantly changing flow of these forces towards the homes of his *nafsu*, his imagination and his thought. For that very reason, if the author is not alert enough, he may easily be influenced by those forces so that, unawares, the content of the story he is writing is distorted; that is to say, a wrong situation is made out to be right and the right one is not even set down.

12. That being so, many scholars remain confused about the content of the story; particularly if the story is intentionally

written in high-flown language, when its entire content will be taken as an empty tale of no significance, even though in fact it may contain much latent meaning.

13. True, the content of many stories does not agree with reality. This may be simply the author's device to prevent the reader seeing clearly all the secrets referred to in the story, or of course it may be to conceal – at the wish and request of the person concerned – the secrets of a person mentioned in the tale.

14. So the reader misunderstands the story and misses its real content. The problem does not of course cause difficulty or surprise to anyone with much experience of the *kejiwaan*. But people lacking such experience may easily guess wrongly and, as well as thinking the incidents of the story really happened, feel a wish arise to imitate it.

15. It is precisely this clouded awareness that causes a person to do something like that mentioned in the story. But what can possibly be gained by imitating someone in the story? Hollowness only – nothing else – making all his painstaking activity utterly meaningless. Hence it is best for you, my children, if you carry out the *latihan* of your inner feeling, as has often been stated earlier – the training, that is, which does not require you to isolate yourselves anywhere nor to abandon all the everyday needs of your life.

16. Rather, this is an easy training, and one that also makes it possible to find a reality where the low forces separate off by themselves. As said many times before, a person can receive this *latihan* of the inner feeling because he embodies the power of the Great Life and because when he begins he is accompanied by someone who has been able to receive this great power previously. In these circumstances, as has also been said, the characteristics of the *nafsu*, the imagination and thought are no longer felt to be influencing the inner feeling.

17. Moreover the form of training to be found therein is not a replica of what other people do, but a specific form that arises spontaneously and is suited and adjusted to the body and its strength.

18. This being so, none of the movements of the *latihan* will harm or damage any part of the body; on the contrary, they can bring health to a person's entire body – something of no little value. In fact what is felt in it is no strange and alien happening, but just an ordinary one that really and truly pertains to mankind eternally.

19. Of course, if you go by your condition at the time of receiving, this really is an extraordinary event, because of the arising of a vibration in the body that finally leads on to movements that suddenly grow stronger and stronger.

20. Further, when this is felt in his body, a man can no longer feel where his thought has gone or where it is situated, and so he feels quite clearly that he has no special desires or aims. Nothing is felt but this emptiness, and the nature of it is just surrender to the Power of God.

21. This makes it clearer that the arising of that movement which encompasses the whole body is not by the wish of the heart and mind. Thus it becomes plainer that, to be able to receive a movement of that kind, a man must find a way by which the tangled forces of thought present in his inner feeling can immediately be set aside.

22. To take this explanation further, after the body makes movements they spread throughout the self until the whole body is aroused like a man waking from sleep. So is it if the man has lived a good life and of course if his forebears too were good.

23. Then he will stand until he receives something like physical exercises or he might make movements like someone dancing gracefully, or worshipping, or behaving like a small child, to the point that to himself it seems a very strange occurrence.

24. In spite of that, it is a pleasant feeling for him; moreover, he is quite conscious in his inner feeling. Eventually the nature of the constantly received movements can be felt and their truth known – that such movements exemplify the true ability of the self.

25. This being so, clearly these movements and behaviour are not without meaning and use, but are the very things that really point to a person's true talent. With their help a man may at length find the way to seek a suitable daily livelihood. This is far different from the kind of movement and activity experienced through mental concentration or through study.

26. The kind of movement one finds happening to one really differs greatly from this latter kind. For the first kind occurs only when a person can truly cancel the power of thought, whereas the second kind is rather the result of concentrating thought or of studying. This makes it clear that the movements and activities that come in the *latihan* never require thought; on the contrary the brain's views and the emotions should be ignored in the inner feeling. This is a necessity to enable a person to surrender everything in the human self to the Greatness of God Almighty.

27. Now about the course of the *latihan* as it continues for others who practise it. Some do not progress so smoothly in their training as their fellows referred to above. The reason for this kind of difference in condition is that before they followed the *latihan*, many of them had acted wrongly; in other words, before they cared to undergo this training of the inner feeling they had often acted wrongly, thus damaging their health. Moreover, this problem is also caused by the faults of their parents.

28. Wrong conduct that began with his forebears and was successively carried down to the man's own self is the precise reason why he now experiences slow progress in the *latihan* and also suffering in his inner feeling.

29. That perhaps makes it clear, so that he will not feel bored at going on with his *latihan* nor choose another way that people sometimes like, such as meditating in a lonely place and eating and sleeping less.

30. Indeed at times people are very fond of doing that sort of thing, believing it can speed up the result wished for. But in practice a person seldom succeeds in achieving his aim. For, clearly, his actions are in truth impelled only by forces still able to mislead his heart and mind. As has been said many times earlier, the position of the heart and mind in the human self is in fact simply that of an ancillary or aide. That is how it is if a person has become able to know his true condition, so that he deliberately chooses to do these things because they are in harmony with his *jiwa*. If, however, it is not like that, will not doing these things only divert him from the direction he wanted to go in? This illustrates the real outcome of an action spurred on by the *nafsu*. So it is best that anything he is going to do should be carefully looked into beforehand.

31. Do understand that a person's body, its content, and his heart and mind are like a lamp, its oil and its flame. Whether in fact the lamp burns well or badly, brightly or dimly, really depends on the quality of the oil in the lamp. So for a man the fine or poor quality of his heart and mind will certainly not be unconnected with the quality of the forces that have become the content of the self.

32. So the main thing is that man should not so readily follow the demands of such a heart and mind. For do understand that if he freely follows the will of his heart and mind, which in reality are still the dupe of the low forces, it is just the same as giving himself into the power of those forces for them to make whatever use of him they please.

33. Especially if his inner feeling and heart and mind have come to be filled by the power of matter. This will be more disastrous still, because then his life in the future will only be of the same quality as that of a material object, for in the slightest event he will act unfeelingly, like a mere thing.

34. Indeed, if the matter has gone so far that no conscious remembrance arises in him of his obligations as a human being, then he will suffer still more in his life, because not only will his outer be blighted but his inner also will experience the same condition.

35. So, then, a man had best go on with the kind of *latihan* he receives, even if his progress may still be called slow. The cause of this slowness – if, my children, you have been able to realize it – is not that he is unfortunate but that it is necessary, so that this gradual progress will not cause damage to the parts of his very sensitive body. Plainly, the *jiwa* has willed this, in fact, because the *jiwa* understands better what degree of strength there is in his self.

36. For its part, the *jiwa* really knows more about the right way to bring a faulty inner feeling back to a good state. This is why the *latihan* is often felt to come to a stop, but to start again not long afterwards, and why too at times movements already experienced recur.

37. It should even be realized, moreover, in order to prevent wrong ideas, that a person often feels in the *latihan* just as though suffering from an illness. And the nature of the illness felt in the *latihan* may not even take the form of just one or two symptoms, but sometimes of many kinds, for they keep changing.

38. The reason for this being felt is that in the past, before doing the *latihan*, the person had suffered much ill-health, and although by the time his inner feeling is being trained his health has evidently come back, yet traces of his illnesses remain within him and so he feels during the *latihan* as though the old days have returned once more. Only, although he feels again a bygone illness, this will do him no harm whatever; rather, it is just by such means that the traces of his ill-health disappear and then a healthy and clean inner feeling really comes into being.

39.   That is why there is no need to be worried about what has been felt in the *latihan*. He should rather give praise and thanks for the Mercy of God because such an event enables his body to become healthy again and his inner feeling clean and pure, so that then he can be active or work in the sphere suitable to his *jiwa*.

40.   So the true nature of their *latihan* is like a well-spring where the inner feeling draws purity instead of dirt, faults and illness. To someone actually suffering an illness this is an event he would never guess at or think of, for by a means evidently so simple his body and inner feeling can be healed and restored to health. But let it not be forgotten that he too, like his fellows mentioned earlier, will have feelings of illness in him during the *latihan*, even rather more, because of course he really is ill.

17
PANGKUR

1. While a person is ill like that, progress in the *latihan* is also slow, as for his fellows referred to earlier.

2. So, then, both someone still unwell and someone already cured will eventually, after receiving slowly in the *latihan*, receive a great deal.

3. At length the movements received encompass the whole body and become orderly: movements, that is, like someone gracefully dancing, doing self-defence exercises, practising sport, or formally praying.

4. Many other kinds of movements too are received time after time in the *latihan*, so the movements a person has had can be used to some extent to observe the low forces that take part in his life and the way they influence his imagination and thought. Despite that, however, his understanding of this matter cannot yet be called complete.

5. For this reason these movements go progressively deeper; in other words, the longer these movements continue the more they are absorbed into the inner feeling, thus making it healthy and clean.

6. When this has happened, those who are following this way then pass on to an inner level where they soon become familiar with a manner of seeing, hearing, smelling, feeling and talking in which the low forces that participate in their life are not taking the lead.

7. And thus they can realize who really has been controlling their capacity to see, hear, smell, feel and speak.

8. Then, when they have received this fully, they can detect where those low forces that take part in their life are located and how they influence the inner feeling, imagination and

thought. At the same time the low forces then spontaneously separate, returning finally to their sources.

9. This means that those that come from the force of matter go back to the force of matter, those that come from the force of vegetation go back to the force of vegetation, those that come from the animal force go back to the animal force, and those that come from the human force go back to the human (*jasmani*) force – although all remain within the human sphere.

10. This done, only then can people fill their original role as organizer and regulator of all the ancillary forces of their life, and only then too can they organize them and get them to co-operate in a perfect family life.

11. Clearly, then, the forces present in the human sphere are not in fact hindrances and obstacles to a man's progress in life; rather, they are cardinal aides to enable him finally to fulfil his tasks and obligations as a high and noble creature.

12. People must therefore be able to organize these forces wisely, in order to guide them to their proper path and so enable them to obtain true satisfaction.

13. In truth the needs of those ancillary forces do not differ from human needs. Like mankind, those forces also need happiness and nobility in their existence. For that reason they need to serve human beings and thus find their right path, so that in the end each returns without difficulty to its own realm.

14. So these forces do not in reality hamper and obstruct the progress of human life; indeed they always obey and follow man's commands.

15. The reason why people can be used as tools of those forces is because people are not able to act rightly as their regulator and organizer; that is to say, in all they do people cannot separate the needs and interests of their ancillary forces from those that belong to their own human self.

16. In such circumstances it is clear that the taproot of all these faults is in a person himself; so is the fruit of these faults. For during his existence he in fact attaches importance only to the life of his *nafsu*, never caring to be aware of the life of his self and of what will happen later on if he cannot become conscious of its content. Yet it is this content of his self that is important to his life, to enable him to stand secure and fulfilled.

17. The principal thing is for this point to be truly understood, so that a man does not become estranged from his ancillary forces and, in his efforts to train his inner feeling, is not required later to lay aside or give up this and that. To sum up, in carrying out any task a man ought not to be separated from his ancillary forces; on the contrary, the truth is that they must be gathered together – though each has its own duties and obligations – to bring about harmonious co-operation in the work he then does. This matter can be likened to someone wishing to build a house: there are the architect, the draughtsman, the foreman, the skilled workmen and the labourers who fetch and carry. For the work to be done properly the architect must not interfere in the labourers' section of the work. Even less fitting is it for the architect to ask for part of the wages for the work he has interfered with. This kind of equality not only leads to imperfect work but can also cause confusion. Moreover, this confusion results in quarrels and struggles for power, and it may easily happen in the end that the architect is removed from his position, so that his place is occupied by the draughtsman or by others from the lowest level, and that the draughtsman is moved to a higher post or even to a lower one perhaps, and his position too is filled by others from the lowest grade.

18. So, to return to the question of a moment ago, it is best for a man not to want to give up or put aside his life aides, for although they may appear to be obstacles, yet only with them can he maintain his high status. On the other hand, if he is unwilling to take notice of their circumstances, these ancillary forces readily become hindrances and obstacles instead, and will greatly hamper him later in whatever he does.

19. Moreover, in reality a man will not be able to rid himself of his ancillary forces, although in his heart he may wish them gone; for of course all these forces have been put in him by the Will of God to make him complete.

20. Hence no matter where a man wants to escape to, he will yet be unable to leave his self behind, nor will it be able to be different from other people's. That is why, when a man wants training for his inner feeling, it is best to look for a way that does not require abandoning all his responsibilities, including his wife and children.

21. By this means a man will not in fact go astray nor believe that he will obtain revelations and salvation on seashore or mountain, for later on that way leads to nothing but bodily illness and added suffering.

22. As stated earlier, that is a way referred to in books of fairy tales, whose truth has yet to be known for sure. For many of the tales told in books embody meanings still secret, and so their truth still needs to be seriously put to the proof. One has to be alert in examining matters of this kind, to enable one in the end to be aware of their correct nature.

23. Now to return to experiences often met in the *latihan* by those being trained. Many of them, after their body has moved a little, soon utter sounds.

24. Gradually the sounds uttered grow stronger until they resemble someone singing, intoning, and so on. After making sounds of that sort some people are even heard to groan like a person asking forgiveness of God Almighty for all his sins. And some of them burst out laughing or cry. At times words are spoken spontaneously as though the person was talking with a friend or somebody else.

25.   Not a few even speak in muddled language and hence feel uneasy or disappointed because they cannot understand its meaning or purpose. Certainly, for those who have only recently started doing the *latihan* this is indeed a thing not easy to understand. For the greater part of what is thus received are words previously brought to utterance by the imagination and mind, but during the *latihan* these words are of necessity cut off from their home in the imagination and mind. So in such circumstances the one receiving will – if he is able to do so – feel that he is like a second person; thus he can tell that the speaker is not in fact his genuine self but another power long embodied in his inner feeling. Clearly, then, most of the words thus spoken are inspired by forces that have appeared in a person's inner feeling. That very fact confirms the truth that the impulse behind most of people's everyday talking comes from forces that have taken charge of their inner feeling. Some things said in the *latihan*, however, are free from the sway of those forces and truly spring from the person's inner self. Usually, however, these are as yet felt feebly, because of course they are expressed by somebody who has not long been opened or been doing the *latihan*. This is why statements are always being received in the *latihan* that conflict with one another. However, a condition of this kind will gradually abate by itself, for the influence of the forces still within the inner feeling will progressively decrease, while, on the other hand, the strong power of his inner self will become increasingly stronger, until at length it is able to rule within him and also to bring into the open the true talent of his *jiwa*.

26.   Of course, in general, such things as that seem strange to those still new to the training, so their attitude to what they receive is still hesitant.

27.   They feel even more astonished if in their *latihan* they are able to utter words to a pleasing beat and tune. At times too some of them can even sing a rhythmic melody which comes from they know not where.

28.   They are still more amazed and bewildered if, after singing such a melody, they then cry and moan over sins they have committed in the past.

29.   When one hears how they cry and lament during the *latihan* it really can grieve one. But, rightly understood, such a state only makes evident their remorse over a self which through heedlessness had come to be used by low forces to do things that are wrong.

30.   For this reason, after the *latihan* they no longer appear troubled. Nevertheless, the experience they undergo penetrates into their inner feeling, with the eventual outcome that, without their willing it, their formerly bad customs and habits change spontaneously and come into accord with the high level of their *jiwa*.

31.   That is the truth of it. So matters of this sort should not be thought about; it is best, rather, just to accept whatever comes next. For progress along the path of the *kejiwaan* cannot be achieved by the power of thought, but only through sincere surrender to the Greatness of God Almighty by way of training the inner feeling, as has been said many times earlier.

32.   Apart from that, the undesirability of using thought does not stop there; it may even cause a confused mental state, with the desire for quick understanding being converted into an experience of continuous inner suffering.

33.   The best course, therefore, for those being trained is just to receive whatever it may be that can be received, for that is the right measure to ensure orderly progress, whereas the desire to speed it up seems useless, for it only afflicts the heart and mind and accomplishes nothing more.

34.   Now to change the subject. Once those being trained receive to the point of being able to utter words, as mentioned above, before long there will usually be added the coming alive of the feelings throughout the body. This will then enable

them little by little to feel aware of the self and of all that actually keeps filling it.

35. Such a state of the self really does not differ from that referred to before, where the forces that fill the human self are always changing, so that its condition is like one in which people are struggling for power. This is the way the forces fill and sway mankind's inner feeling. When anybody is heedless of his state he will easily be misled by them.

36. From there on the person taking the training begins gradually to be introduced to the nature of those forces and also to perceive the way they associate with him. Truly, those forces are there, in the human self, only to serve man's needs, and their nature is indeed only that of aides. But if people, for their part, are not yet able to assume their rightful being, then the forces whose nature is that of aides reverse things and take charge.

37. So, through the manifesting of the life force which has been experienced in the *latihan* – and which is beyond the scope of thought – a man will soon be able to feel how those forces separate from and combine with his true being in the inner feeling. His state will then be the same as when, in receiving the *latihan*, he utters all sorts of words, as has been described – that is to say, he becomes like a second person.

38. That state will become progressively firmer until at last he will have the habit of separating from and combining with those ancillary forces. Looked at with the mind, this really is an astonishing event, but for someone fortunate enough to be able to have insight into the *kejiwaan*, of the kind mentioned a little way back, doubtless such a thing no longer seems strange to his self.

39. Then, after the one being trained has received clearly about those ancillary forces separating from and combining with his true being, he will be able to feel more and more

113

clearly how those forces influence the inner feeling and so arouse the *nafsu* of greed, anger, patience and acceptance.

40.   He can also feel how those forces lure a person into taking great pleasure in the taste of the food he eats – which is also their way of deluding him into doing something wrong.

41.   More important still, a man is also able to feel how he is lured into a great liking for sexual intercourse. So he gains much and is at length enabled to separate his inner self from the stream of forces that have such a bad influence on his inner feeling; likewise, little by little he finds how to open the way for those forces to flow towards their proper goal. Given this condition, in sexual union with his wife he will at length be able to unite the content of the inner feeling of both natures, male and female.

42.   Such is the opportunity awaiting him. So, at the time of union with his wife, he must first get used to the way of separating the inner self from the influence of those forces.

43.   Having taken that step, he will grow progressively more deft and clear in doing it, with the result that in sexual union with his wife he can become a vessel into which can descend a content – the seed of a perfect human being.

44.   This content, the seed of a perfect human being, means the content that will in time form a noble nature and that will also produce the kind of character which is of real value to the life and way of life of man and society.

45.   Thus the state of the child later on, both outwardly and inwardly, will be far different from that of his parents who, from the time they began the training until so long afterwards, had to endure inner suffering and to have complete patience.

46.   Fortunately they were able to face this problem before it was too late, and so could soon undertake the training of their inner feeling, even though they felt that they could not make quick headway. Blessed, however, by the firmness of

their inner feeling, they could yet attain in the end what they wished for.

47. It is even usual after a time that, while someone is experiencing the *latihan*, a state also arises in which he begins to be able to smell out how the ancillary forces of human life make him want to smell all sorts of smells.

48. Here the state of the person being trained is just the same as that already mentioned: he seems like two people. Thus he can be aware of what comes from his inner self and what has been aroused by the ancillary forces of human life.

49. This becomes increasingly clear for those being trained, until they are aware of the reason why people get pleasure from smelling smells and also why people differ in their liking for smells.

50. From experience like this in the *latihan* it will also become clear to them how somebody truly is who is making up to them. For that reason also, then, it is necessary for them in their *latihan* to be able to separate the stream of the ancillary forces of human life from those whose source is their inner self, in order that after separation the forces may go on to flow spontaneously in their rightful directions.

18
PUCUNG

1. Thinking should not be used for this purpose, because a man cannot possibly understand it with that faculty; indeed, if his inner feeling is not really firm, the mind will easily be agitated.

2. Much the best thing, then, is for this to be done only by means of the *latihan* of the inner feeling – frequently referred to earlier – because it is a way easy to attain.

3. It really is very easily attained, provided a man does nothing in practice that conflicts with what has been explained above.

4. For in reality the *latihan* is already one with his inner feeling, so that all he needs is to be vigilant.

5. So while smelling something a man should be really aware of what is experienced.

6. For a number of forces join in at the time of smelling, so if a man is inattentive, even for just a moment, then he will instantly become unable to tell one from another of the forces that impose on his inner feeling at such a time.

7. That being so, he cannot possibly distinguish between the pressure of the human force coming from himself and the pressure from his ancillary forces. On the other hand, however, if fully alert he will be able to tell the difference between them.

8. When he has managed to do this, the relationship between himself and his ancillary forces will be like that in a family, with the man as its head while his ancillary forces are like servants or employees intended to support his position in life.

116

9.   It has been so willed in life that man should occupy the highest place. Rightly, then, man must be capable of thus regulating the flow of those forces in his inner feeling.

10.   This means that he must be able to channel each of them in the direction of their rightful goal, so that their condition is one of working together towards the eternal life, which can bring happiness both to mankind and to each of those forces.

11.   Such is the benefit obtained by people who have become skilled at organizing the flow of ancillary forces present in their inner feeling. It will be no surprise, then, if in the end they are quickly able to discover the nature of their own needs.

12.   This enables them to be very clearly conscious of the role of those forces in the human inner feeling.

13.   Only after that does a man realize that in everything he does – when smelling something, for example – his ancillary forces take part.

14.   And so in that way he will become more familiar with how mankind's ancillary forces blend within the inner feeling.

15.   He will also be able to realize what is the nature of the desire of those forces for something they want.

16.   Later he will be able to recognize the differences between the desires of each force, and so come to know his condition accurately, even though those forces mix in his actions at every step.

17.   A man really learns a great deal then, so that at length he can spontaneously channel the flow of those forces in their rightful directions.

18.   That is why, if a man is still without any understanding of this, his inner feeling and his heart and mind are very easily influenced by mankind's ancillary forces.

19. And, unawares, the man just follows the cupidity of those forces, of which the one that influences the human inner feeling most is the power of matter.

20. So it is. Very different, then, is the man who already understands about forces mixing in the human inner feeling. To this man none of those forces any longer impedes or influences the inner feeling; they will have found their own path pointing towards the goal that is rightfully theirs.

19

MEGATRUH

1. Now to vary the discussion: to explain further how mankind's ancillary forces operate in the various organs or members of the body, it is well to add to what has been explained before.

2. Man's ancillary forces also blend within his inner feeling when he hears any sound or voice.

3. They race one another to reach the heart and mind.

4. The winner of the race immediately enters the inner feeling and unites with the whole of it, thus turning into the person's desire.

5. The one that most usually and perhaps most easily can reach man's heart and mind is the force of matter: that is, the force of things that appear dead and that move only because of man.

6. In such circumstances, my children, you must therefore feel thoroughly the different ways in which these forces influence the inner feeling, and feel in what state each of them is after it has separated from your own will – that is, from your own human will.

7. The way they influence the inner feeling until at length they manifest in man's hearing does not differ from what has been said above.

8. That being so, my children, you must be alert to be able really to feel the working of each of the forces in your hearing, and the shifting of their various pleasures and enthusiasms, so that later you can understand their individual characters.

9. Now something else must be explained: in the same way as you experience the receiving just mentioned, you

will also be able to feel how man's ancillary forces take part in seeing.

10.   Likewise you will be able to tell how those forces mix in your feeling while you are tasting food and speaking; moreover, you will also be able to notice them blend within your feeling when you experience inner bliss.

11.   Thus has God willed life to be. Those forces are indeed destined to be man's aides, so one may well say that they are with man in life and death. Only, you need to become conscious of them, so that during your life you may thereby receive how to direct the work of each of them.

12.   That really is most important for you, my children, because when those forces within you have been regulated your status as a human being will spontaneously be strengthened, and you will be able to know and supervise the work and the use of each of those ancillary forces.

13.   That is why in the *latihan* you need to feel accurately what happens with those forces.

14.   By succeeding in this you will find the way opening for you of itself, my children, so that you can easily set your course towards perfection.

15.   The meaning of perfection is that you as human beings will have found the inner purpose that is your own, or is genuine. With this you will no longer feel like a man's body empty of the unsuspected power that arouses the inner feeling so that it can become an instrument for receiving understanding that will be of benefit to human life on earth and hereafter.

16.   Such are the truths to be learnt from this training, enabling you to act with clear knowledge of your own role and with an awareness of life that does not ignore the Greatness of God Almighty.

17. You will know and understand, my children, the limits of the desires and of the abilities of each of those forces; likewise you will be able to be conscious of the ability and purpose of your own real self.

18. Then in that state it will feel as if the forces have become separated from one another, though in reality they are all mixed together in the way sugar is mixed with its sweetness.

19. Once you have reached that stage, the truth is that those forces will feel satisfied, for the simple reason that each will have been able to find the course that is certainly its rightful direction.

20. Nor will your own proper self receive less, so that you will be able to feel really sure that your steps and your path will be unimpeded.

20
DHANDHANGGULA

1.   That being so, then you will soon become adept at doing work that is in tune with your *jiwa*, and this will certainly make your life happy, for this skill will stem or grow from your human *jiwa*, which will have brought to life your whole inner feeling. So it is, my children; hence your zeal for your work will persist and your progress or advance in it will not be disappointing.

2.   That is what is truly called culture, for its source is the human *jiwa* and it is received in an inner feeling that has risen free of the sway of the ancillary forces. It is a culture filled continuously with the life force. That is why the work you do will be a means for your worship of the Almighty.

3.   Seen from an ordinary or outer viewpoint, the nature of your work will not differ from that of normal work, but in reality it will be far different. For ordinary work and skill are acquired by learning from someone else – or from a group – unable yet to determine whether or not the work is in harmony with one's identity. But the skill in work that you will acquire is of a quality whose source, as previously explained, is the human *jiwa*.

4.   Later, therefore, in doing your work, your outer and inner can never be otherwise than in accord, and so you will certainly progress in your work in harmony with the advances and changes of the times you live in.

5.   That is how it is, my children; so it is to be hoped that you will not come to forget the *latihan kejiwaan*, for truly it is a way easy to follow and not requiring you to isolate yourself from your fellow men, and it will also easily bring you real results that can strengthen your being.

6. Thereby you will really gain a great deal, enabling you readily, without strain, to satisfy the needs that are most fitting for you.

7. Moreover, by this means your existence will always be enveloped by a life force that is beyond fathoming by the mind, so that you will easily find the path that will broaden the scope of your life.

8. Plainly, then, the skill in work acquired through the *latihan kejiwaan* is truly a quality of genuine culture, for of course it is born and grows because the human *jiwa* has become free of all the influence of man's ancillary forces. So for that reason this culture will neither destroy human knowledge nor close the way to man's worship of the Almighty, but rather is another requirement of that worship, for in reality of course it comes from God and thus to God it returns.

9. So this writing ends, closing with simply this hope: may those who are on this way follow the training of the inner feeling zealously; and may they also be able to receive the Grace of God Almighty, so that in time they may sincerely show the way to those who are interested in the *latihan* of the inner feeling.

Contact Addresses

For those wishing to make contact with Subud, the following is a list of addresses current at the time of printing:

Subud Britain: Brecon Subud Centre, Walton Villa, Brecon, Powys LD3, Wales. Tel: (44) 0874 623110.

Subud USA: B701 Bel-Red Road, Suite B, Bellevue, WA 98005, USA. Tel: (1) 206 643 1904

Subud Canada: PO Box 92, Station H, Toronto, Ontario, Canada, M4C 5H8.

Subud Australia: 8 Elder Street, Clayton South, Victoria 3169, Australia. Tel: (61) 3 551 4307.

Subud New Zealand: 4/6 Curran Street, Herne Bay, Auckland, NZ. Tel: (69) 9 606 834.

Subud South Africa: PO Box 487, Melville 2109, South Africa. Tel: (27) 11 726 2024.

International Subud Committee: Takatsu, PO Box 40, Kawasaki-shi, Japan 213. Tel: (81) 44 877 1162.